✳ At a Glance

Reader

D0115012

✳ At a Glance

Reader

SECOND EDITION

Lee Brandon
Mt. San Antonio College

Houghton Mifflin Company   *Boston   New York*

To Sharon

Publisher: Patricia A. Coryell
Senior Sponsoring Editor: Lisa Kimball
Senior Development Editor: Judith Fifer
Editorial Associate: Peter Mooney
Project Editor: Shelley Dickerson
Manufacturing Coordinator: Chuck Dutton
Senior Marketing Manager: Annamarie Rice
Marketing Assistant: Andrew Whitacre

Cover image: © Ablestock

Acknowledgments and credits appear on page 190, which constitutes an extension of the copyright page.

Printed in the U.S.A.

Library of Congress Control Number: 2004115528

ISBN-10: 0-618-54229-9
ISBN-13: 978-0-618-54229-1

3456789 – MP – 13 12 11 10 09

✳ Contents

✳ Readings Grouped by Patterns of Writing

Analysis by Division

Process Analysis

Cause and Effect

Classification

Comparison and Contrast

Definition

Argument

Literary Analysis

✳ Preface

At a Glance: Reader is the fourth book in the *At a Glance* series of concise English textbooks. Along with *At a Glance: Sentences, At a Glance: Paragraphs,* and *At a Glance: Essays,* it meets the current need for succinct, comprehensive, and up-to-date textbooks that students can afford. All four books provide basic instruction, exercises, and writing assignments at the designated level, as well as support material for instructors. *At a Glance: Sentences* and *At a Glance: Paragraphs* include a transition to the next level of writing, while *At a Glance: Paragraphs, At a Glance: Essays,* and *At a Glance: Reader* end with a handbook to which students can refer for help with sentence-level issues or problems with mechanics.

    At a Glance: Reader includes basic writing instruction with its thirty reading selections and can be used alone, with one of the other *At a Glance* books, or with another textbook. Two or more *At a Glance* books can be shrink-wrapped and delivered at a discount.

✳ Features

Essential, comprehensive information in a concise format to produce an economical textbook.

Readings
- Thirty engaging sources on the following eleven themes:

xiii

Chapter 12: Fast Food Workers: Robots or Thinkers?
Chapter 13: Bullies 'R' Us?

- More than 90 percent of the reading selections new to this edition.
- Guide questions for discussion and critical thinking with each essay.
- Suggested topics for writing in response to individual reading selections and thematic groups appear at the end of each chapter.

Writing Instruction

- Discussion of the writing process, including a student writing demonstration.
- Directions for documented writing.
- A description and explanation of writing patterns and combined patterns, with suggested general topics.
- A handbook covers sentence-level issues, including sentence types, sentence combining, sentence problems (fragments, comma splices, run-ons), sentence variety, omissions, wordiness, punctuation, and capitalization.
- A Writing Process Worksheet guides students through the stages of composition.
- *At a Glance* student website at http://college.hmco.com/devenglish/student and other Houghton Mifflin support.

Reading Instruction

- Basic instruction for underlining, outlining, and annotating reading material.

✳ Support Material for Instructors

- *At a Glance* instructor website at http://college.hmco.com/devenglish/instructor: Answers to exercises; reproducible diagnostic tests, sentence-writing quizzes, and reading quizzes; sample syllabus to adopt or adapt for different course designs; PowerPoint slides that can be downloaded and used to enhance classroom instruction.
- *At a Glance* student website at http://college.hmco.com/devenglish/student: Additional exercises; additional readings; a brief discussion of APA and MLA styles; instructions for writing résumés and letters of application; suggestions for taking tests.

- Software resources include updated Expressways 5.0 CD-ROM, interactive software that guides students as they write and revise paragraphs and essays; Houghton Mifflin Grammar CD-ROM; American Heritage Dictionary CD-ROM.
- Online options include Dolphinville, an online writing center, and SMARTHINKING, live online tutoring and academic support by trained e-instructors.

❊ Acknowledgments

I am profoundly indebted to the following instructors who have reviewed this textbook: Don Brotherton, DeVry University; Richard Greene, Florida Community College at Jacksonville; Alison Kuehner, Ohlone College; and Dr. Susanne Linden Seidel, Nassau Community College. Thanks also to members of the English Department at Mt. San Antonio College.

I deeply appreciate the work of freelance permissions editor Mary Dalton Hoffman, and Nancy Benjamin of Books By Design, as well as my colleagues at Houghton Mifflin: Lisa Kimball, Judy Fifer, Annamarie Rice, Shelley Dickerson, Andrew Whitacre, and Peter Mooney.

I am especially grateful to my family of wife, children and their spouses, and grandchildren for their cheerful, inspiring support: Sharon, Kelly, Erin, Kathy, Michael, Shane, Lauren, Jarrett, and Matthew.

Lee Brandon

✳ Student Overview

At a Glance: Reader is an affordable book with basic reading instruction, concise writing instruction, and thirty reading selections chosen to make you sometimes grin, sometimes laugh, sometimes wince, sometimes growl, sometimes bristle, and always think. Immediate benefits of its use should include lively classroom discussion and thoughtful writing responses. Your reading-related writing may be evaluations, comparative studies, arguments for or against, or your own somewhat parallel experiences.

Chapter 1 will help you use the writing process for a natural flow of thought. Chapter 2 will help you with organization if you need to write essays that are mainly patterns such as comparison and contrast, cause and effect, argument, or process analysis. The Appendix is a handbook that will help you with sentence-level writing: sentence types, sentence combining, sentence problems (fragments, comma splices, run-ons), sentence variety, omissions, wordiness, punctuation, and capitalization.

The readings in this book include essays, book excerpts, short stories, and ballads. Review the table of contents and see the themes around which the selections are grouped and note the range of subject material that awaits your reading and reactions.

✳ Linking Reading and Writing

Following are some strategies to help you make the best use of this book and jump-start your reading and writing skills.

1. **Be active and systematic in learning.** Take advantage of your instructor's expertise by being an active participant in class—one who takes notes, asks questions, and contributes to discussion. Become dedicated to systematic learning: determine your needs, decide what to do, and do it. Make learning a part of your everyday thinking and behavior.

2. **Read widely.** Read to learn technique, to acquire ideas, to be stimulated to write. Especially read to satisfy your curiosity and to receive pleasure. If reading is a main component of your course, approach it as systematically as you do writing.

3. **Keep a journal.** Keeping a journal may not be required in your particular class, but whether required or not, it is a good idea to jot down your own ideas. Here are some ideas for daily, or regular, journal writing:

   - Summarize, evaluate, or react to reading assignments.
   - Summarize, evaluate, or react to what you see on television and in movies, and to what you read in newspapers and magazines.
   - Describe and narrate situations or events you experience.
   - Write about career-related matters you encounter in other courses or on the job.

   Your journal entries may read like an intellectual diary, a record of what you are thinking about at certain times. Because your entries are not structured writing assignments, organization and editing are not important. Mainly, keeping a journal will help you to understand the material you read, to develop your language skills, to think more clearly, to become more confident, and to write more easily—so that writing itself becomes a comfortable, everyday activity. Your entries may also provide subject material for longer, more carefully crafted pieces. The most important thing is to get into the habit of writing something each day.

4. **Evaluate your writing skills.** Use the Self-Evaluation Chart inside the front cover of this book to list areas you need to work on. You can add to your lists throughout the entire term. Drawing on your instructor's comments, make notes on matters such

as the organization, development, and content of your essays, spelling, vocabulary, and diction, and so on. Use the chart for self-motivated study assignments and as a checklist in all stages of writing. As you master each problem area, you can check it off or cross it out.

Here is a partially filled out Self-Evaluation Chart, with some guidelines for filling out your own.

Self-Evaluation Chart

Organization/ Development/ Content	Spelling/ Vocabulary/ Diction	Grammar/ Sentence Structure	Punctuation/ Capitalization
Avoid top-heavy intro-ductions 5 Use specific examples 18 Repeat key words such as *causes* and *effects* 2	all right 3 separate 3 sophomore 3 avoid "into" as in "into rap" 2 "couldn't care less" 2	Vary sentence beginnings 170 Watch for pronoun-antecedent problems, such as "a person . . . they" 171 RO/CS—*Then* isn't a conjunc-tion 167	comma after long introductory modifier 183 colon to introduce list 186 cap beginning for words replacing names, such as, "I told Mother," but "I told my mother" 188

Organization/Development/Content. Note your instructor's suggestions for all aspects of planning your essays and supporting your ideas.

Spelling/Vocabulary/Diction. List words marked as incorrectly spelled on your assignments. Master the words on your list and add new words as you accumulate assignments. List suggestions made by your instructor about word choice (such as avoiding slang, clichés, and vague terms). Also include new, useful words you encounter in this class and others; add the words here, with simple definitions. Use another page if you need more space.

Grammar/Sentence Structure. List any grammar points you need to remember or any sentence problems, such as fragments, comma splices, and run-ons. If you tend to begin sentences in the same way or to use the same patterns, use your chart to remind yourself to vary your sentence beginnings and patterns.

Punctuation/Capitalization. List any problems you encounter with punctuation or capitalization.

5. **Use the Writing Process Worksheet.** Record details about each of your assignments, such as the due date, topic, length, and form. The worksheet will also remind you of the stages of the writing process: explore, organize, and write. A blank Writing Process Worksheet for you to enlarge and photocopy for assignments appears on page xxi.

6. **Be positive.** Don't compare yourself with others. Compare yourself with yourself, and as you make progress, consider yourself what you are—a student on the path toward effective writing, a student on the path toward success.

Writing Process Worksheet

Title _____

Name _____ Due Date _____

Assignment   In the space below, write whatever you need to know about your assignment, including information about the topic, audience, pattern of writing, length, whether to include a rough draft or revised drafts, and whether your paper must be typed.

Stage One   **Explore** Freewrite, brainstorm (list), cluster, or take notes as directed by your instructor. Use separate paper if you need more space.

Stage Two   **Organize** Write a topic sentence or thesis; label the subject and treatment parts.

Write an outline or a structured list.

Stage Three   **Write** On separate paper, write and then revise your paragraph or essay as many times as necessary for **c**oherence, **l**anguage (usage, tone, and diction), **u**nity, **e**mphasis, **s**upport, and **s**entences (**CLUESS**). Read your work aloud to hear and correct any grammatical errors or awkward-sounding sentences.

Edit any problems in fundamentals, such as **c**apitalization, **o**missions, **p**unctuation, and **s**pelling (**COPS**).

✳ 1

Writing Paragraphs and Essays

✳ The Writing Process: Prewriting

1. The writing process consists of strategies that can help you produce a polished essay. **Prewriting** includes exploring, experimenting, gathering information, writing the controlling idea, and organizing and developing support. **Writing** includes drafting, revising, and editing.

2. Prewriting covers one or more of the following strategies:

   Freewriting: writing without stopping so that you can explore, experiment, and invent

   Brainstorming or listing: responding to *Who? What? Where? When? Why?* and *How?* questions or making lists on likely divisions of your subject

   Clustering: showing related ideas by double-bubbling a subject and then connecting single bubbles of related ideas on spokes radiating out and branching from the hub

   Gathering information: underlining, annotating, and note taking

   Composing the topic sentence or thesis: writing a sentence that has two parts—the subject (what you are writing about) and the treatment (what you will do with the subject)

   Outlining: dividing the controlling idea into sections of support material, dividing those sections further, and establishing a workable sequence

✳ The Writing Process: Writing, Revising, and Editing

1. **Writing**
   Write your first draft, paying close attention to your outline or list or cluster. Do not concern yourself with perfect spelling, grammar, or punctuation.

2. Revising

Use the acronym CLUESS: coherence, language, unity, emphasis, support, sentence structure.

Coherence

- Are the ideas clearly related, each one to the others, and to the central idea?
- Is there a clear pattern of organization (time, space, or emphasis)?
- Is the pattern supported by words that suggest the basis of that organization (time: *now, then, later*; space: *above, below, up, down*; emphasis: *first, second, last*)?
- Is coherence enhanced by the use of transitional terms, pronouns, repetition, and a consistent point of view?

Language

- Is the general style of language usage appropriate (properly standard and formal or informal) for the purpose of the piece and the intended audience?
- Is the tone (language use showing attitude toward material and audience) appropriate?
- Is the word choice (diction) effective? Do the words convey precise meaning? Are they fresh and original?

Unity

- Are the thesis and every topic sentence clear and well stated? Do they indicate both subject and treatment?
- Are all points of support clearly related to and subordinate to the topic sentence of each paragraph and to the thesis of the essay?

Emphasis

- Are ideas properly placed (especially near the beginning and end) for emphasis?
- Are important words and phrases repeated for emphasis?

Support

- Is there adequate material—such as examples, details, quotations, and explanations—to support each topic sentence and the thesis?
- Are the points of support placed in the best possible order?

Sentence Structure

- Are the sentences varied in length and beginnings?
- Are the sentences varied in pattern (simple, compound, complex, and compound-complex)?
- Are all problems with sentence structure (fragments, comma splices, run-ons) corrected?

3. **Editing**

- Are all problems in such areas as capitalization, omissions, punctuation, and spelling (COPS) corrected?

✳ The Paragraph and Its Parts

1. The **developmental paragraph** is a group of sentences, each with the function of stating or supporting a controlling idea called the **topic sentence.**
2. The developmental paragraph contains three parts: the subject, the topic sentence, and the support.
3. The two main patterns of the developmental paragraph are these:

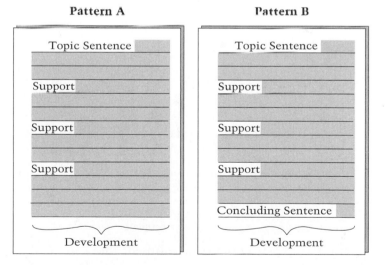

Pattern A

Topic Sentence

Support

Support

Support

Development

Pattern B

Topic Sentence

Support

Support

Concluding Sentence

Development

4. The topic sentence includes what you are writing about—the **subject**—and what you intend to do with that subject—the **treatment.**

<u>Being a good parent</u> <u>is more than providing financial support.</u>
　　　subject　　　　　　　　　　　　treatment

5. The **outline** is a pattern for showing the relationship of ideas. It can be used to reveal the structure and content of something you read or to plan the structure and content of something you intend to write. The following topic outline shows how the parts are arranged on the page as well as how the ideas in it relate to one another.

Main Idea (will usually be the topic sentence for the paragraph or the thesis for the essay)
  I. Major support
    A. Minor support
      1. Details (specific information of various kinds)
      2. Details
    B. Minor support
      1. Details
      2. Details
 II. Major support
    A. Minor support
    B. Minor support
      1. Details
      2. Details
      3. Details
Concluding sentence (optional)

✳ The Essay and Its Parts

1. An **essay** is a group of paragraphs, each of which supports a controlling statement called a **thesis.**
2. An effective thesis has both a subject and a treatment.

The **subject** is what you intend to write about.
The **treatment** is what you intend to do with your subject.

<u>Bidwell Elementary School</u> <u>is too crowded.</u>
　　　　subject　　　　　　　　　treatment

3. An effective thesis presents a treatment that can be developed with supporting information.
4. An ineffective thesis is vague, too broad, or too narrow.

5. Each paragraph in an essay is almost always one of three types: introductory, support, or concluding.

6. A good **introductory paragraph** attracts the reader's interest, states or points toward the thesis, and moves the reader smoothly into the support, or body, paragraphs.

7. Introductory methods include a direct statement of the thesis, background, definition of term(s), quotation(s), a shocking statement, question(s), and a combination of two or more methods in this list.

8. **Supporting paragraphs,** also called **developmental paragraphs,** are often presented in patterns, such as narration, cause and effect, analysis by division, and process analysis.

9. The **concluding paragraph** should give the reader the feeling that you have said all you want to say about your subject.

10. Some effective methods of concluding are a restatement of the thesis in slightly different words, perhaps pointing out its significance or making applications of it; a review of the main points; an anecdote related to the thesis; and a quotation.

The essay can often be considered an amplification of a developmental paragraph.

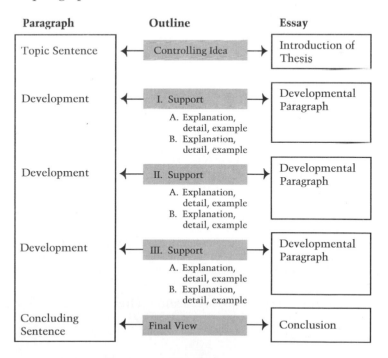

✳ Reading-Related Writing

Because most college writing assignments are connected with reading, it is worthwhile to consider how to focus thoughtful attention on the written word. Of course, if you know about writing assignments or tests beforehand, your reading can be more concentrated. You should always begin a reading assignment by asking yourself why you are reading that particular material and how it relates to your course work and interests. For example, most selections in this book are presented as ideas to stimulate thought and invite reflective comparisons, to provide material for analysis and evaluation, and to show how a pattern or process of writing can be done effectively. The discussion and critical-thinking questions and activities that follow the selections arise from these purposes. Other questions raised by your instructor or on your own can also direct you in purposeful reading. Consider such questions and activities at the outset. Then, as you read, use the following strategies that are appropriate for the kind of assignment you are working on:

1. *Underlining* helps you to read with discrimination.

   - Underline the main ideas in paragraphs.
   - Underline the support for those ideas.
   - Underline answers to questions that you bring to the reading assignment.
   - Underline only the key words.

2. *Annotating* enables you to actively engage the reading material.

   - Number parts if appropriate.
   - Make comments according to your interests and needs.

3. *Outlining* the passages you read sheds light on the relationship of ideas, including the major divisions of the passage and their relative importance.

4. *Summarizing* helps you concentrate on main ideas. A summary

   - cites the author and title of the text.
   - is usually shorter than the original by about two-thirds, although the exact reduction will vary depending on the content of the original.
   - concentrates on the main ideas and includes details only infrequently.

- changes the original wording without changing the idea.
- does not evaluate the content or give an opinion in any way (even if you see an error in logic or fact).
- does not add ideas (even if you have an abundance of related information).
- does not include any personal comments by the author of the summary (therefore, no use of *I* referring to self).
- seldom uses quotations (and then, only with quotation marks).
- uses some author tags ("says York," "according to York," or "the author explains") to remind the reader(s) that you are summarizing the material of another writer.

Two other types of reading-related writing are

- The **reaction**—explains how the reading relates to you, your experiences, and your attitudes; also, it often is your critique of the worth and logic of the piece.
- The **two-part response**—presents a summary separate from a reaction.

This excerpt includes underlining and annotation by Vincent Sheahan for his reading-related essay on pages 9–13.

It was a long time before I began thinking mechanistically enough to accept migraine for what it was: **Chronic** something with which I would be living, the way some people live with diabetes. Migraine is something more than the fancy of a neurotic imagination. **Hereditary** It is an essentially hereditary complex of symptoms, the most frequently noted but by no means the **Main** most unpleasant of which is a vascular headache of **symptom** blinding severity, suffered by a surprising number of women, a fair number of men (Thomas Jefferson had migraine, and so did Ulysses S. Grant, the day he accepted Lee's surrender), and by some unfortunate children as young as two years old. . . . Almost any- **Trigger** thing can trigger a specific attack of migraine: stress, **varies—** allergy, fatigue, an abrupt change in barometric pres- **for me** sure, a contretemps over a parking ticket. A flashing **too—** light. A fire drill. One inherits, of course, only the predisposition. In other words I spent yesterday in

| Only my uncle? | bed with a headache not merely because of my bad attitudes, unpleasant tempers and wrongthink, but because both my grandmothers had migraine, my father has migraine and my mother has migraine. |

—Joan Didion, In Bed

✳ Informal Documentation

Documenting is giving credit to borrowed ideas and words. If you are writing in response to material in your textbook, especially if it is a single source, your instructor may not require you to indicate by page number where you found each borrowed idea. However, you will be expected to make clear (by use of quotation marks and by the name of an author, the title of the selection, or both name and title) that you have borrowed ideas. Simply writing something such as "I agree with Suzanne Britt when she says in 'Neat People vs. Sloppy People' that disorganized people have good intentions" would suffice. This style of acknowledgment is commonly called *informal documentation*. It is often used in college writing when both writer and readers have familiarity with and shared access to the sources. Informal documentation also is common in newspaper and periodical articles.

✳ Formal Documentation

Documenting sources for papers based on written material is usually quite simple. One popular documentation method is MLA (Modern Language Association) style. Here are its most common principles that can be used for textbook or other restricted sources, with some examples.

- If you use material from a source you have read, identify that source so that the reader will recognize it or be able to find it.
- Document any original idea borrowed, whether it is quoted, paraphrased (written in your words but not shorter), or summarized (written in your words and shorter). Basic situations include the following:

> Normally, you need give only the author's name and a page number: (Rivera 45).
>
> If you state the author's name in introducing the quotation or idea, then usually give only the page number: (45).

If the author has written more than one piece referenced in the book, then a title or shortened form of the title is also required: (Rivera, *The Land* 45).

Here is an example of documenting a quotation by an author represented only once in a textbook.

- Using the author's name to introduce:

  Suzanne Britt says that "neat people are bums and clods at heart" (255).

Following is an example of documenting an idea borrowed from an author but not quoted.

- Using the author's name to introduce:

  Suzanne Britt believes that neat people are weak in character (255).

- Not using the author's name to introduce:

  Music often helps Alzheimer's patients think more clearly (Weiss 112).

✳ Demonstration: Student Essay

My-graines

Vincent Sheahan

The assignment was to read an essay related to health and write a documented essay of extended definition about a health condition as it related to the student's experience. (Your instructor may not ask you to formally document an essay based on a single source found in your textbook; instead, clear references and accurate use of quotations marks would suffice.)

1   The aura set in like a suffocating stillness before a tropical storm. "This is going to be a bad one," I told myself as I shut off the lights, took medication, lay down, and prepared for the inevitable--the relentless throbbing in my temple. About three

hours of incapacitating agony later, I recovered, feeling strangely drained, and skimmed through my reading assignment for my college English class. What a coincidence! It included "In Bed," an essay about migraines by Joan Didion. Because I had only recently been diagnosed with migraines (although I had long suffered), I naturally had enormous curiosity about the subject, and now homework coincided

Thesis with my private need for information. <u>By closely comparing my family history, my triggers for attacks, and my personality with Joan Didion's, perhaps I could find some informed answers to my questions and be able to define "migraines" more precisely.</u>

2   A year ago when I decided to seek medical

Topic <u>help, the matter of family history was of
sentence immediate concern.</u> At my first appointment, my neurologist informed me that, although no one knows why, migraines tend to run in families. I said the only person in my family who has migraines is my Uncle Joe, my father's brother. For Didion, the family connection is more apparent and pervasive: Both of her grandmothers, her father, and her mother all suffer from migraine headaches. But she does go on to explain, "One inherits,

of course, only the predisposition" (59).
Therefore, it is possible that everyone on my
father's side has carried the gene for
migraines but only Uncle Joe has developed
the headaches.

3

Topic sentence

After the doctor asked his questions, I
had one of my own: What actually causes
migraine headaches? I was fearful that my job
as an emergency medical technician (E.M.T.),
with its debilitating stress and irregular
hours, was the main reason. He explained that
the exact causes are not completely
understood and that my fatigue and irregular
sleep patterns are not the causes of my
migraines, because there are plenty of
E.M.T.'s who have the same sleep patterns as
I do, yet do not have migraines. Nevertheless,
the fatigue and irregular sleep may trigger
migraine headaches. For Didion, the triggers
are varied. She says, "Almost anything can
trigger a specific attack of migraine:
stress, allergy, fatigue, an abrupt change in
barometric pressure, a contretemps over a
parking ticket. A flashing light. A fire
drill" (60). Yet she explains that her
headaches are not triggered at times when she
needs to be alert and thinking clearly, such

as an emergency situation, but instead, they are triggered when she is feeling overwhelmed or extremely stressed (60).

4

Topic sentence

In addition to the exposure to these triggers, a migraine sufferer like me usually has what is called a "migraine personality." Didion offers a good definition of that term, saying that she is typical, a perfectionist who is "ambitious, inward, intolerant of error, rather rigidly organized" (60). But she points out that not all perfectionists have migraines and not all people with migraines are perfectionists. She says that she is a perfectionist about writing, not housekeeping (60). And as for me, I try-- probably harder than most--to be organized when it comes to my education, work, and personal life.

5

Like Joan Didion, I am intensely interested in migraines, and I am learning about them. We migraine sufferers have much in common, though each of us has his or her own family history of migraines, triggers, and migraine personality. Knowing that others go through what I do and having more information about my condition make it easier for me to deal with the pain of my migraines. I will continue to do the same thing Joan

> Didion does when she has an aura: I won't try
> to fight it. I will lie down and endure. When
> it's finally over, I will count my blessings.

Vincent Sheahan's instructor asked him to include a citation of his source in MLA form. It is annotated to indicate parts.

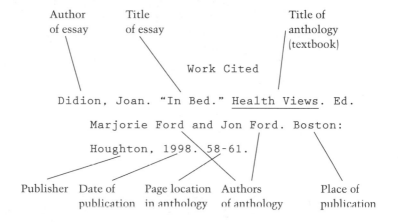

Author of essay   Title of essay   Title of anthology (textbook)

Work Cited

Didion, Joan. "In Bed." Health Views. Ed.
Marjorie Ford and Jon Ford. Boston:
Houghton, 1998. 58-61.

Publisher   Date of publication   Page location in anthology   Authors of anthology   Place of publication

Here is the same MLA form applied to a source from this textbook.

Gallagher, Joyce. "The Messy Are in Denial." *At a Glance: Reader.* Ed. Lee Brandon. Boston: Houghton, 2006. 76–79.

2

Combined and Specific Patterns of Writing

✳ Combined Patterns of Writing

Organization in a sound paragraph or essay reflects the intention of the author in fulfilling the needs of a writing task. As that writer, you begin by asking yourself what you are trying to say and who your audience is. If you are attempting to compare and contrast subject material, such as generations or leaders, then a comparative pattern of writing will prevail, providing a framework for your thoughts. If your objective is to show the causes of something, perhaps a trend or an event, then a discernible pattern of causes is likely to emerge in your writing.

Patterns can help you organize your thoughts so that your audience can easily understand your message. Each pattern is a collection of strategies for achieving certain purposes. Patterns are especially useful at the workplace when you need to respond succinctly according to a company-honored format or in a college essay test when your work must be done with an oppressive clock ticking and evaluated by instructors overloaded with bluebooks.

Two cautionary points are worth considering.

- If the strategies are used in a strictly formulaic manner, the result may be mechanical and uninteresting. Fleshing out your ideas with explanation will usually submerge patterns of writing.
- It is uncommon for a single pattern to be used alone, and you would seldom attempt to do so. You cannot write a comparison-and-contrast essay without analyzing your content through division, and you might very well use definitions and examples.

Therefore, a well-written essay is usually a combination of different patterns from the ten or so available to you in narrative, descriptive, expository, and persuasive writing. One form may very well provide the organizational plan for your writing, but it should not be mechanical.

This chapter presents basic strategies for using those patterns, including some general writing topics that can be used to practice the patterns. In the following chapters connecting reading with writing, some suggested reading-related writing assignments will cross-reference directions in this chapter. For example, if a suggested assignment is clearly specifying how to do something, the parenthetical cross-reference will give the page number(s) for strategies on writing a paper of process analysis.

✳ Specific Patterns of Writing

Narration

1. Include these points so that you will be sure you have a complete narrative:

   - situation (what's going on)
   - conflict (problem to be dealt with)
   - struggle (dealing with problem)
   - outcome (result of dealing with problem)
   - meaning (significance or point)

2. Use these techniques or devices as appropriate:

   - images that appeal to the senses (sight, smell, taste, hearing, touch) and other details to advance action
   - dialogue (conversation)
   - transitional devices (such as *next, soon, after, later, then, finally, when, following*) to indicate chronological order

3. Give details concerning action.
4. Be consistent with point of view (use *I* for first person or *he, she,* or *it* for third person) and verb tense (use *is* for present and *was* for past).
5. Keep in mind that most narratives written as college assignments will have an expository purpose; that is, they explain a specific idea.
6. Consider working with a limited time frame for short writing assignments. That is, the scope would usually be no more than one incident of brief duration for one paragraph. For example, writing about an entire graduation ceremony might be too complicated, but concentrating on the moment when you walked forward to receive the diploma or the moment when the relatives and friends come down on the field could work very well in a single paragraph.

General Topics

Each of the following topics concerns the writing of a narrative with meaning beyond the story itself. The narrative will be used to inform or to persuade in relation to a clearly stated idea.

1. Write a narrative based on a topic sentence such as this: "One experience showed me what _____ [pain, fear, anger, love, sacrifice, dedication, joy, sorrow, shame, pride] was really like."
2. Write a simple narrative about a fire, a riot, an automobile accident, a rescue, shoplifting, or some other unusual happening you witnessed.
3. Write a narrative that supports (or opposes) the idea of a familiar saying such as one of the following:

   You never know who a friend is 'til you need one.
   A bird in the hand is worth two in the bush.
   A person who is absent is soon forgotten.
   Nice people finish last.
   It's not what you know, it's whom you know.
   Fools and their money are soon parted.
   Every person has a price.

Description

1. **Description** is the use of words to represent the appearance or nature of something in either an objective or a subjective manner.
2. Effective **objective description** presents the subject clearly and directly as it exists outside the realm of feelings.

   - For objective description—for example, a biology lab report—use direct, practical language appealing mainly to the sense of sight.

3. Effective **subjective description** is also concerned with clarity and it may be direct, but in addition it conveys a feeling about the subject and sets a mood while making a point.

   - For subjective description, appeal to the reader's feelings, especially through images of sight, sound, smell, taste, and touch.

4. Instead of using general, abstract words, consider using specific, concrete words to enhance your description.

   - *Food* is general; *Oreo cookie* is specific.
   - *Beauty* is abstract; *sunset* is concrete.

5. Apply these questions to your writing:

- What is the dominant impression I am trying to convey?
- What details support the dominant impression?
- What is the primary order of the details as I present them: time or place?
- What is the point of view? Am I avoiding needless shifts by using either the first-person (*I*) or the third-person (*he, she, it, they*) perspective? Am I as the writer involved in what I describe?

6. Consider giving your description a narrative framework (situation, conflict, struggle, outcome, significance).

General Topics

Be sure to keep your purpose and audience in mind, as you determine whether your description will be objective or subjective.

Objective Description

1. A visible part of your body, such as a toe, a finger, an ear, a nose, or an eye
2. A construction, such as a building, room, desk, chair, or table
3. A mechanism, such as a bicycle, wagon, car, motorcycle, CD player, can opener, or stapler

Subjective Description

4. Personalize a trip to a supermarket, a stadium, an airport, an unusual house, a mall, a beach, a courtroom, a house of worship, a club, a business, a library, or a police or fire station. Describe a simple conflict in one of those places while emphasizing descriptive details.

   Pick a high point in any event and describe the most important few seconds. Consider how the scene can be captured by a video camera and then give the event focus by applying the dominant-impression principle, using relevant images of sight, sound, taste, touch, and smell. The event might be a ball game, graduation or wedding ceremony, funeral, dance, concert, family gathering, class meeting, rally, riot, robbery, fight, proposal, or meal. Limit your subject material to what you can cover effectively in the passage you write.

Exemplification

1. Use examples to explain, convince, or amuse.
2. Use examples that are vivid, specific, and representative.

   - Vivid examples (the most colorful or memorable from your list of possible examples) attract attention.
   - Specific examples (such as names of places, things, and people) are identifiable.
   - Representative examples (those that are recognizable to readers) are typical and therefore the basis for generalization.

3. Tie your examples clearly to your thesis and your main points.
4. Draw your examples from what you have read, heard, and experienced.
5. Brainstorm a list or cluster of possible examples before you write.
6. Choose the order (time, place, or emphasis) and number of your examples according to the purpose stated in your topic sentence or thesis.

General Topics

Make a judgmental statement about an issue you believe in strongly and then use one or more examples to illustrate your point. These are some possible topics:

1. The price of groceries is too high.
2. Professional athletes are paid too much.
3. A person buying a new car may get a lemon.
4. Drivers sometimes openly ignore the laws on a selective basis.
5. Politicians should be watched.
6. Working and going to school is tough.
7. Working, parenting, and going to school is tough.
8. All computer viruses have common features.
9. Many people under the age of eighteen spend too much time playing computer games.
10. Some computer games teach children useful skills.

Analysis by Division

Almost anything can be analyzed by division—for example, how the parts of the ear work in hearing, how the parts of the eye work in seeing, or how the parts of the heart work in pumping blood throughout the body. Subjects such as these are all approached with the same systematic procedure.

1. This is the procedure.

   - Step 1: Begin with something that is a unit.
   - Step 2: State the principle by which the unit can function.
   - Step 3: Divide the unit into parts according to that principle.
   - Step 4: Discuss each of the parts in relation to the unit.

2. This is the way you might apply that procedure to a good boss.

   - Unit: Manager
   - Principle of function: Effective as a leader
   - Parts based on the principle: Fair, intelligent, stable, competent in field
   - Discussion: Consider each part in relation to the person's effectiveness as a manager.

3. This is how a basic outline of analysis by division might look.

   Thesis: To be effective as a leader, a manager needs specific qualities.

   I. Fairness

   II. Intelligence

   III. Stability

   IV. Competence in the field

General Topics

Some of the following topics are too broad for a short writing assignment and should be narrowed. For example, the general "a wedding ceremony" could be narrowed to the particular: "José and Maria's wedding ceremony." Divide your focused topic into parts and analyze it.

1. A machine such as an automobile, a computer, a camera
2. A city administration, a governmental agency, a school board, a student council
3. A wedding, graduation, or religious ceremony
4. A holiday celebration, a pep rally, a sales convention, a religious revival
5. An offensive team in football (any team in any game)
6. A family, a relationship, a gang, a club, a sorority, a fraternity
7. An album, a performance, a song, a singer, an actor, a musical group, a musical instrument
8. A movie, a television program, a video game
9. Any well-known person—athlete, politician, criminal, writer

Process Analysis

1. Decide whether your process analysis is mainly **directive** (how to do something) or **informative** (how you did something or how something occurred). Be consistent in using pronouns and other designations.

   - For the directive process analysis, use the second person, addressing the reader as *you*. The *you* may be understood, even if it is not written.
   - For the informative process analysis, use the first person, speaking as *I* or *we*, or the third person, speaking about the subject as *he, she, it,* or *they*, or by name.

2. Consider using these basic forms.

Directive Process Analysis

I. Preparation	How to Prepare Spring Rolls
A.	I. Preparation
B.	A. Suitable cooking area
II. Steps	B. Utensils, equipment
A.	C. Spring-roll wrappers
B.	D. Vegetables, sauce
C.	II. Steps
	A. Season Vegetables
	B. Wrap vegetables
	C. Fold wrappers
	D. Deep fry rolls
	E. Serve rolls with sauce

Informative Process Analysis

I. Background	How Coal Is Formed
A.	I. Background or context
B.	A. Accumulation of land
II. Sequence	plants
A.	B. Bacterial action
B.	C. Muck formation
C.	II. Sequence
	A. Lignite from pressure
	B. Bituminous from deep burial
	and heat
	C. Anthracite from metamorphic conditions

3. Listing is a useful prewriting activity for this form. Begin with the Roman-numeral headings indicated in item 2.
4. The order of a process analysis will usually be chronological (time based) in some sense. Certain transitional words are commonly used to promote coherence: *first, second, third, then, soon, now, next, finally, at last, therefore,* and *consequently.*

General Topics

Most of the following topics are directive as they are phrased. However, each can be transformed into a how-it-was-done informative topic by personalizing it and explaining stage by stage how you, someone else, or a group did something. For example, you could write either a directive process analysis about how to deal with an obnoxious person or an informative process analysis about how you or someone else dealt with an obnoxious person. Keep in mind that the two types of process analysis are often blended, especially in the personal approach. Many of the following topics will be more interesting to you and your readers if they are personalized.

Select one of the following topics and write a process-analysis paragraph or essay about it. Most of the topics require some narrowing to be treated in a paragraph. For example, writing about playing baseball is too broad; writing about how to throw a curve ball may be manageable.

1. How to end a relationship without hurting someone's feelings
2. How to pass a test for a driver's license
3. How to get a job at_____
4. How to eat_____
5. How to perform a magic trick
6. How to repair_____
7. How to assemble_____
8. How to learn about another culture
9. How to approach someone you would like to know better

Cause and Effect

1. Determine whether your topic should mainly inform or mainly persuade, and use the right tone for your purpose and audience.
2. Use listing to brainstorm cause-and-effect ideas. This is an effective form for prewriting.

Causes	Event, Situation, or Trend	Effects
Low self-esteem	*Joining a gang*	Life of crime
Drugs		Drug addiction
Tradition		Surrogate family
Fear		relationship
Needs surrogate family		Protection
Wants protection		Ostracism
Neighborhood status		Restricted vocational
		opportunities

3. Decide whether to concentrate on causes, effects, or a combination of causes and effects. Most paragraphs will focus only on causes or only on effects. Many short essays will discuss causes and effects but will use one as the framework for the piece. A typical basic outline might look like this:
   Topic sentence of paragraph or thesis of essay

   I. Cause (or Effect) 1
   II. Cause (or Effect) 2
   III. Cause (or Effect) 3

4. Do not conclude that something is an effect merely because it follows something else. For example, a recession after the election of a new leader may or may not be an effect of the election.
5. Lend emphasis to your main concern(s)—causes, effects, or a combination—by repeating key words such as *cause, reason, effect, result, consequence,* and *outcome.*
6. Causes and effects can be primary (main) or secondary (contributing), immediate or remote.
7. The order of causes and effects in your paper may be based on time, space, emphasis, or a combination.

General Topics

Select one of the topics in the following list as a subject (situation, circumstance, or trend) for your paragraph or essay and then determine whether you will concentrate on causes, effects, or a combination. You can probably write a more interesting, well-developed, and therefore successful paragraph or essay on a topic you can personalize. For example, a discussion about a specific young person who contemplated, attempted, or committed suicide is probably a better topic idea than a general discussion of suicide. If you do not personalize the topic, you will probably have to do some basic research to supply details for development.

1. Attending or completing college
2. Having or getting a job
3. Change in policy or administration
4. Change in coaches, teachers, officeholder(s)
5. Alcoholism
6. Gambling
7. Moving to another country, state, or home
8. Exercise
9. Passing or failing a test or course
10. Popularity of a certain television program or song
11. Early marriage

Classification

1. Follow this procedure for writing paragraphs and essays of classification:

   - Select a plural subject.

     neighbors

   - Decide on a principle for grouping the units of the subject.

     involvement in neighborhood

   - Establish the classes (groups).

     I. Friendly

     II. Meddlesome

     III. Private

2. Avoid uninteresting phrases for your classes, such as *good/average/bad, fast/medium/slow,* and *beautiful/ordinary/ugly.*
3. Avoid overlapping classes.

   I. Friendly

   II. Meddlesome

   III. Private

   IV. Wealthy (Any of the first three could be wealthy.)

4. Use Roman numeral headings to indicate classes.

   I. Class 1

   II. Class 2

   III. Class 3

5. If you use subclasses, clearly indicate the different levels.

    I. Friendly

   II. Meddlesome

  III. Private

      A. Shy

      B. Smug

      C. Strange

6. Following your outline, give somewhat equal (however much is appropriate) space to each class.

General Topics

Write a paragraph or an essay using one of the topics listed here. Divide your topic into groups according to a single principle.

1. Intelligence
2. Waitresses
3. Dates
4. Smokers
5. Smiles
6. Liars
7. Gossips
8. TV watchers
9. Clothing styles
10. Sports
11. Dopers
12. Sports fans
13. Churchgoers
14. Laughs
15. Bus drivers
16. Bus or airplane passengers
17. Junk food
18. Graffiti
19. Home computers
20. Mothers or fathers
21. Rock music
22. Telephone talkers
23. Pick-up lines (as in a bar)
24. Chicken eaters
25. Surfers (Internet or ocean)
26. Beards
27. Pet owners

Comparison and Contrast

One useful procedure for writing comparison-and-contrast paragraphs and essays is using the 4 *P*'s: *purpose, points, patterns,* and *presentation.*

1. **Purpose:** During the exploration of your topic, define your purpose clearly.

   - Decide whether you are writing a work that is primarily comparison, primarily contrast, or balanced.
   - Determine whether your main purpose is to inform or to persuade.
   For example, you might argue that one minivan is better than another.

2. Points

- Indicate your points of comparison or contrast, perhaps by listing.
- Eliminate irrelevant points.

(horsepower and gears)

(safety)

style

price

comfort

(cargo space)

3. Pattern

- Select the subject-by-subject or the point-by-point pattern after considering your topic and planned treatment. The point-by-point pattern is usually preferred in essays. Only in long papers is there likely to be a mixture of patterns.
- Compose an outline reflecting the pattern you select.

Subject-by-Subject Pattern

I. Subject 1
    A. Point 1
    B. Point 2
II. Subject 2
    A. Point 1
    B. Point 2

I. Nissan Quest
    A. Horsepower and gears
    B. Safety
    C. Cargo space
II. Dodge Caravan
    A. Horsepower and gears
    B. Safety
    C. Cargo space

Point-by-Point Pattern

I. Point 1
    A. Subject 1
    B. Subject 2
II. Point 2
    A. Subject 1
    B. Subject 2
III. Point 3
    A. Subject 1
    B. Subject 2

I. Horsepower and gears
    A. Nissan Quest
    B. Dodge Caravan
II. Safety
    A. Nissan Quest
    B. Dodge Caravan
III. Cargo space
    A. Nissan Quest
    B. Dodge Caravan

4. Presentation

- Be sure to give each point more or less equal treatment. Attention to each part of the outline will usually ensure balanced development.
- Use transitional words and phrases to indicate comparison and contrast and to establish coherence.
- Use a carefully stated topic sentence for a paragraph and a clear thesis for an essay. Each developmental paragraph should have a topic sentence broad enough to embrace its content.

General Topics

Make these topics specific by naming the subjects for your comparison and contrast.

1. Two products, such as automobiles, bicycles, motorcycles, snowmobiles
2. Two types of (or specific) police officers, doctors, teachers, clergy, students, athletes
3. Living at college and living at home
4. A small college and a large college, or a four-year college and a community college
5. Two roommates, neighbors, friends, dates
6. Two movies, television shows, commercials, songs, singers
7. Dating and going steady, living together and being married, a person before and after marriage
8. Shopping malls and neighborhood stores
9. Two department stores, such as Wal-Mart and Kmart

Definition
Simple Definition

1. No two words have exactly the same meaning.
2. Several forms of simple definitions can be blended into your discussion: basic dictionary definitions, synonyms, direct explanations, indirect explanations, and analytical definitions.
3. For a formal or analytical definition, specify the term, class, and characteristic(s).

Example <u>Capitalism</u> <u>is an economic system</u> <u>characterized by investment</u>
       term   class
       <u>of money, private ownership, and free enterprise.</u>
                 characteristics

4. Avoid "is where" and "is when" definitions, circular definitions, and the use of words in the definition that are more difficult than the word being defined.

Extended Definition

1. Use clustering to consider how you might use other patterns of development in defining your term. (See page 28.)
2. The organization of your extended definition is likely to be one of emphasis, but it may also be one of space or time, depending on the subject material. You may use just one pattern of development for the overall organization.
3. Consider these ways of introducing a definition: with a question, with a statement of what it is not, with a statement of what it originally meant, or with a discussion of why a clear definition is important. You may use a combination of these ways before you continue with your definition.
4. Whether you personalize a definition depends on your purpose and your audience. Your instructor may ask you to write about a word within the context of your own experience or to write about it from a detached, clinical viewpoint.

General Topics

The following topics are appropriate for extended development of definitions; most of them will also serve well for writing simple definitions.

1. Conservative	11. Clotheshorse	21. School spirit
2. Asian American	12. Educated	22. Feminist
3. Bonding	13. Gang	23. Chicano
4. Sexist	14. Freedom	24. Jock
5. Cult	15. Body language	25. Hispanic American
6. Biker	16. Hero	26. African American
7. Liberal	17. Druggie	27. Macho
8. Workaholic	18. Convict	28. Cool
9. Surfer	19. Teen slang	29. Native American
10. Personal space	20. Psychopath	30. Jerk

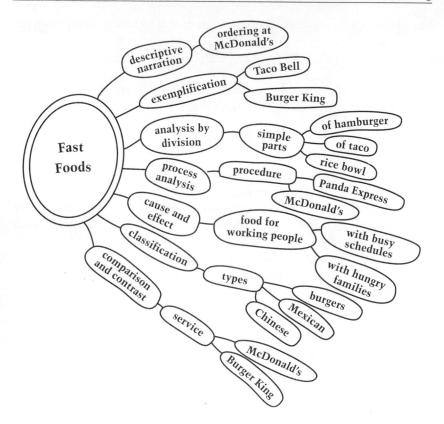

Argument

1. Ask yourself the following questions. Then consider which parts of the formal argument you should include in your paragraph or essay.

   - **Background:** What is the historical or social context for this controversial issue?
   - **Proposition** (the **thesis** of the essay): What do I want my audience to believe or to do?
   - **Qualification of proposition:** Can I limit my proposition so that those who disagree cannot easily challenge me with exceptions?
   - **Refutation** (taking the opposing view into account, mainly to point out its fundamental weakness): What is the view on the other side, and why is it flawed in reasoning or evidence?

- **Support:** In addition to sound reasoning, can I use appropriate facts, examples, statistics, and opinions of authorities?

2. The basic pattern of a paragraph or an essay of argument is likely to be in this form:

Proposition (the thesis of the essay)
   I. Support 1
  II. Support 2
 III. Support 3

General Topics

The following are broad subject areas; you will have to limit your focus for an essay of argument. You may modify the topics to fit specific situations.

1. Sexual harassment
2. Juvenile justice
3. Endangered-species legislation
4. Advertising tobacco
5. Homelessness
6. State-run lotteries
7. Jury reform
8. Legalizing prostitution
9. Censoring rap or rock music
10. Cost of illegal immigration
11. Installation of local traffic signs
12. Foot patrols by local police
13. Change in (your) college registration procedure
14. Local rapid transit
15. Surveillance by video (on campus, in neighborhoods, or in shopping areas)
16. Zone changes for stores selling liquor
17. Curfew for teenagers
18. Laws keeping known gang members out of parks

Literary Analysis

1. In analyzing a piece of literature, consider its setting, conflict, characters, plot, point of view, and especially its theme. You would usually emphasize one of those aspects.
2. Writing about literature may be analytical (as in point 1), or it may be more speculative, personal, or comparative.

3. Develop your ideas by referring directly to the story; by explaining; and by using summaries, paraphrases, and quotations.
4. Use the present tense in relating events in the story.
5. Use quotation marks correctly around the words you borrow.
6. For organization, consider patterns of development such as analysis by division, comparison and contrast, and cause and effect.

3

Chapters from the Book of Love

Love is probably easier to experience than to define. Some would say that, like jazz, if you have to ask what it means you wouldn't understand the answer. In a recent study, college students were asked to list the different kinds of love. They named 216, including friendship, parental, brotherly, sisterly, romantic, sexual, spiritual, obsessive, possessive, and puppy love.

This chapter about love may help you come up with your own definition and list. This is something only you can do, for love is personal. Don't bother with scholarly research. Your Google search engine, in all its cyberspace glory, cannot tell you even who wrote the Book of Love.

The following five reading selections will connect your heart and brain to this topic that makes the world go round and the birds and bees create birdlets and beelets.

- "How Do I Love Thee?" defines.
- "Romantic Love, Courtship, and Marriage" brings sociology to the issue.
- "Why Marriages Fail" probes Cupid's psyche.
- "The Story of an Hour" offers sixty minutes of liberation from love.
- "The Ballad of Anna Banana" transports our topic to a poignant, earthy realm in a ballad that asks the age-old musical question "Have I told you lately that I love you?"

How Do I Love Thee?

Robert J. Trotter

> *How one loves depends on many things, including who is loving and who is being loved, but each love has certain components. Robert Trotter, using the system developed by R. J. Sternberg, details the different types of love by giving explanations and providing examples.*

1   Intimacy, passion, and commitment are the warm, hot, and cold vertices of Sternberg's love triangle. Alone and in combina-

tion they give rise to eight possible kinds of love relationships. The first is nonlove—the absence of all three components. This describes the large majority of our personal relationships, which are simply casual interactions.

2   The second kind of love is liking. "If you just have intimacy," Sternberg explains, "that's liking. You can talk to the person, tell about your life. And if that's all there is to it, that's what we mean by liking." It is more than nonlove. It refers to the feelings experienced in true friendships. Liking includes such things as closeness and warmth but not the intense feelings of passion or commitment.

3   If you just have passion, it's called infatuated love—the "love at first sight" that can rise almost instantaneously and dissipate just as quickly. It involves a high degree of physiological arousal but no intimacy or commitment. It's the tenth-grader who falls madly in love with the beautiful girl in his biology class but never gets up the courage to talk to her or get to know her, Sternberg says, describing his past.

4   Empty love is commitment without intimacy or passion, the kind of love sometimes seen in a 30-year-old marriage that has become stagnant. The couple used to be intimate, but they don't talk to each other any more. They used to be passionate, but that's died out. All that remains is the commitment to stay with the other person. In societies in which marriages are arranged, Sternberg points out, empty love may precede the other kinds of love.

5   Romantic love, the Romeo and Juliet type of love, is a combination of intimacy and passion. More than infatuation, it's liking with the added excitement of physical attraction and arousal but without commitment. A summer affair can be very romantic, Sternberg explains, but you know it will end when she goes back to Hawaii and you go back to Florida, or wherever.

6   Passion plus commitment is what Sternberg calls fatuous love. It's Hollywood love: Boy meets girl, a week later they're engaged, a month later they're married. They are committed on the basis of their passion, but because intimacy takes time to develop, they don't have the emotional core necessary to sustain the commitment. This kind of love, Sternberg warns, usually doesn't work out.

7   Companionate love is intimacy with commitment but no passion. It's a long-term friendship, the kind of committed love and intimacy frequently seen in marriages in which the physical attraction has died down.

8   When all three elements of Sternberg's love triangle come together in a relationship, you get what he calls consummate love, or complete love. It's the kind of love toward which many people strive, especially in romantic relationships. Achieving consummate love, says Sternberg, is like trying to lose weight, difficult but not impossible. The really hard thing is keeping the weight off after you have lost it, or keeping the consummate love alive after you have achieved it. Consummate love is possible only in very special relationships.

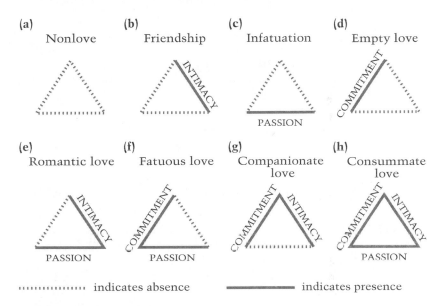

(a) Nonlove   (b) Friendship   (c) Infatuation   (d) Empty love

(e) Romantic love   (f) Fatuous love   (g) Companionate love   (h) Consummate love

·············· indicates absence   ▬▬▬▬▬▬ indicates presence

Exercise 1 Discussion and Critical Thinking

1. What are the eight different types of love described by Trotter?

2. What examples does Trotter use? Which ones are general and which are specific? What additional examples can you think of, taken from what you have read and what you have seen in movies and on television?

3. What are some specific examples of the types of love for which Trotter does not provide his own examples?

Romantic Love, Courtship, and Marriage

Ian Robertson

> *Romantic love, courtship, and marriage are more than matters of the heart. According to Ian Robertson, they are all perfectly understandable parts of our culture, and they do not exist in the same way outside our culture. In this excerpt from his college textbook,* Sociology, *Robertson explains the causes of our loving, courting, and marrying. He says that, often without thinking about what we are doing, we respond to the needs of both society and ourselves.*

Romantic Love

1   The American family is supposed to be founded on the romantic love of the marital partners. Traces of a more pragmatic attitude persist in the American upper classes, where daughters are expected to marry "well"—that is, to a male who is eligible by reason of family background and earning potential. Most Americans, however, tend to look askance at anyone who marries for money or some other practical reason in which love plays no part.

2   Happily enough, romantic love defies a clinical definition. It is a different kind of love, though, from the love you have for your parents or your dog. It involves physical symptoms, such as pounding heart and sexual desire, and psychological symptoms, such as obsessive focus on one person and a disregard for any resulting social or economic risks. Our culture encourages us to look for this love—to find that "one and only," perhaps even through "love at first sight." The phenomenon of romantic love occurs when two people meet and find one another personally and physically attractive. They become mutually absorbed, start to behave in what may appear to be a flighty, even irrational manner, decide that they are right for one another, and may then enter a marriage whose success is expected to be guaranteed by their enduring passion. Behavior of this kind is portrayed and warmly endorsed throughout American popular culture, by books, magazines, comics, records, popular songs, movies, and TV.

3   Romantic love is a noble idea, and it can certainly help provide a basis for the spouses to "live happily ever after." But since marriage can equally well be founded on much more practical considerations, why is romantic love of such importance in the modern world? The reason seems to be that it has the fol-

lowing basic functions in maintaining the institution of the nuclear family.

4   1. *Transfer of loyalties.* Romantic love helps the young
partners to loosen their bonds with their family of orientation, a
step that is essential if a new neolocal nuclear family is to be
created. Their total absorption in one another facilitates a transfer of commitment from existing family and kin to a new family of procreation, something that would be unlikely to happen
under the extended family system.

5   2. *Emotional support.* Romantic love provides the couple
with emotional support in the difficulties that they face in establishing a new life of their own. This love would not be so
necessary in an extended family, where the relatives are able to
confront problems cooperatively. In an extended family, in fact,
romantic love might even be dysfunctional, for it could distract
the couple from their wider obligations to other kin.

6   3. *Incentive to marriage.* Romantic love serves as a bait to
lure people into marriage. In the extended family system of traditional societies, it is automatically assumed that people will
marry, but in the modern world, people have considerable choice
over whether they will get married or not. A contract to form a
lifelong commitment to another person is not necessarily a very
tempting proposition, however: to some, the prospect may look
more like a noose than like a bed of roses. Without feelings of romantic love, many people might have no incentive to marry.

7   To most of us, particularly to those who are in love, romantic love seems to be the most natural thing in the world, but sociological analysis shows that it is a purely cultural product,
arising in certain societies for specific reasons. In a different
time or in a different society, you might never fall in love, nor
would you expect to.

Courtship and Marriage

8   A courtship system is essentially a marriage market. (The
metaphor of the "market" may seem a little unromantic, but in
fact, the participants do attempt to "sell" their assets—physical
appearance, personal charms, talents and interests, and career
prospects.) In the matter of mate selection, different courtship
systems vary according to how much choice they permit the individual. The United States probably allows more freedom of
choice than any other society. A parent who attempts to inter-

fere in the dating habits or marriage plans of a son or daughter is considered meddlesome and is more likely to alienate than persuade the young lover.

9   In this predominantly urban and anonymous society, young people—often with access to automobiles—have an exceptional degree of privacy in their courting. The practice of dating enables them to find out about one another, to improve their own interpersonal skills in the market, to experiment sexually if they so wish, and finally to select a marriage partner.

10   Who marries whom, then? Cupid's arrow, it turns out, does not strike at random. Despite the cultural emphasis on love as something mysterious and irrational, the selection of marital partners is more orderly and predictable than romantics might like to think. In general, the American mate-selection process produces *homogamy*, marriage between partners who share similar social characteristics. Among the characteristics that seem to attract people to one another are the following:

11   1. *Similar age.* Married partners tend to be of roughly the same age. Husbands are usually older than their wives, but this difference in age has been gradually declining throughout the century, from about 4 years in 1900 to 2.4 years today.

12   2. *Social class.* Most people marry within their own social class. The reasons are obvious: we tend to live in class-segregated neighborhoods, to meet mostly people of the same class, and to share class-specific tastes and interests. Interclass marriages are relatively more common, however, among college students. When there are class differences in a marriage, it is most often the wife who marries upward.

13   3. *Religion.* Most marriages are between people sharing the same religious faith, although Protestant interdenominational marriages are fairly common. Many people change their religion to that of their partner before marriage.

14   4. *Education.* Husbands and wives generally have a similar educational level. The college campus is, of course, a marriage market in its own right, and college-educated people are especially likely to marry people who have a similar education achievement.

15   5. *Racial and ethnic background.* Members of racial and ethnic groups are more likely to marry within their own group than outside it. In particular, interracial marriages are extremely rare. Until the 1960s, several states had laws prohibiting interracial marriages, and such marriages still attract some

social disapproval. Interracial marriages between blacks and whites are particularly unusual; in the majority of these cases, the husband is black and the wife white.

16   6. *Propinquity.* Spatial nearness is a common feature of those who marry one another, for the obvious reason that people are likely to have more social interaction and similarities with neighbors, coworkers, or fellow students than with others who are physically more distant.

Exercise 2 Discussion and Critical Thinking

1. What is the subject (a situation, circumstance, or trend) at the center of this discussion?

2. Is this piece concerned mainly with causes, effects, or a combination?

3. What are the three cultural needs or causes (also called functions) that make romantic love useful in American society?

4. How would you rank the three functions of romantic love in order of importance?

5. On the basis of what assets do individuals attempt to sell themselves on the "marriage market"?

6. Why do people fall in love? What six causes (or characteristics) does Robertson list?

7. Which of the six causes (characteristics) do you think are the most important?

8. Are the assets or the characteristics more important? Should they be? Why or why not?

Why Marriages Fail

Anne Roiphe

> *As a novelist and journalist, Anne Roiphe has been especially concerned with the topic of contemporary relationships. In this essay, first published in* Family Weekly, *she concentrates on two phenomena all too frequently linked: marriage and divorce.*

1   These days so many marriages end in divorce that our most sacred vows no longer ring with truth. "Happily ever after" and "Till death do us part" are expressions that seem on the way to becoming obsolete. Why has it become so hard for couples to stay together? What goes wrong? What has happened to us that close to one-half of all marriages are destined for the divorce courts? How could we have created a society in which 42 percent of our children will grow up in single-parent homes? If statistics could only measure loneliness, regret, pain, loss of self-confidence and fear of the future, the numbers would be beyond quantifying.

2   Even though each broken marriage is unique, we can still find the common perils, the common causes for marital despair. Each marriage has crisis points and each marriage tests endurance, the capacity for both intimacy and change. Outside pressures such as job loss, illness, infertility, trouble with a child, care of aging parents and all the other plagues of life hit marriage the way hurricanes blast our shores. Some marriages survive these storms and others don't. Marriages fail, however, not simply because of the outside weather but because the inner climate becomes too hot or too cold, too turbulent or too stupefying.

3   When we look at how we choose our partners and what expectations exist at the tender beginnings of romance, some of the reasons for disaster become quite clear. We all select with unconscious accuracy a mate who will recreate with us the emotional patterns of our first homes. Dr. Carl A. Whitaker, a marital therapist and emeritus professor of psychiatry at the University of Wisconsin, explains, "From early childhood on each of us carried models for marriage, femininity, masculinity, motherhood, fatherhood, and all the other family roles." Each of us falls in love with a mate who has qualities of our parents, who will help us rediscover both the psychological happiness and miseries of our past lives. We may think we have found a man unlike Dad, but then he turns to drink or drugs, or loses his job over and over again or sits silently in front of the TV just the way Dad did. A man may choose a woman who doesn't like

kids just like his mother or who gambles away the family savings just like his mother. Or he may choose a slender wife who
seems unlike his obese mother but then turns out to have other
addictions that destroy their mutual happiness.

4   A man and a woman bring to their marriage bed a blended
concoction of conscious and unconscious memories of their
parents' lives together. The human way is to compulsively repeat and recreate the patterns of the past. Sigmund Freud so
well described the unhappy design that many of us get trapped
in: the unmet needs of childhood, the angry feelings left over
from frustrations of long ago, the limits of trust and the recur-
rence of old fears. Once an individual senses this entrapment,
there may follow a yearning to escape, and the result could be a
broken, splintered marriage.

5   Of course people can overcome the habits and attitudes that
developed in childhood. We all have hidden strengths and amazing capacities for growth and creative change. Change, however,
requires work—observing your part in a rotten pattern, bringing
difficulties out into the open—and work runs counter to the
basic myth of marriage: "When I wed this person all my problems will be over. I will have achieved success and I will become the center of life for this other person and this person will
be my center, and we will mean everything to each other for-
ever." This myth, which every marriage relies on, is soon ex-
posed. The coming of children, the pulls and tugs of their demands on affection and time, place a considerable strain on that
basic myth of meaning everything to each other, of merging together and solving all of life's problems.

6   Concern and tension about money take each partner away
from the other. Obligations to demanding parents or still-
dependent-upon parents create further strain. Couples today
must also deal with all the cultural changes brought on in recent years by the women's movement and the sexual revolu-
tion. The altering of roles and the shifting of responsibilities
have been extremely trying for many marriages.

7   These and other realities of life erode the visions of marital
bliss the way sandstorms eat at rock and the ocean nibbles
away at the dunes. Those euphoric, grand feelings that accom-
pany romantic love are really self-delusions, self-hypnotic
dreams that enable us to forge a relationship. Real life, failure at
work, disappointments, exhaustion, bad smells, bad colds and
hard times all puncture the dream and leave us stranded with

our mate, with our childhood patterns pushing us this way and that, with our unfulfilled expectations.

8   The struggle to survive in marriage requires adaptability, flexibility, genuine love and kindness and an imagination strong enough to feel what the other is feeling. Many marriages fall apart because either partner cannot imagine what the other wants or cannot communicate what he or she needs or feels. Anger builds until it erupts into a volcanic burst that buries the marriage in ash.

9   It is not hard to see, therefore, how essential communication is for a good marriage. A man and a woman must be able to tell each other how they feel and why they feel the way they do; otherwise they will impose on each other roles and actions that lead to further unhappiness. In some cases, the communication patterns of childhood—of not talking, of talking too much, of not listening, of distrust and anger, of withdrawal—spill into the marriage and prevent a healthy exchange of thoughts and feelings. The answer is to set up new patterns of communication and intimacy.

10   At the same time, however, we must see each other as individuals. "To achieve a balance between separateness and closeness is one of the major psychological tasks of all human beings at every stage of life," says Dr. Stuart Bartle, a psychiatrist at the New York University Medical Center.

11   If we sense from our mate a need for too much intimacy, we tend to push him or her away, fearing that we may lose our identities in the merging of marriage. One partner may suffocate the other partner in a childlike dependency.

12   A good marriage means growing as a couple but also growing as individuals. This isn't easy. Richard gives up his interest in carpentry because his wife, Helen, is jealous of the time he spends away from her. Karen quits her choir group because her husband dislikes the friends she makes there. Each pair clings to each other and is angry with each other as life closes in on them. This kind of marital balance is easily thrown as one or the other pulls away and divorce follows.

13   Sometimes people pretend that a new partner will solve the old problems. Most often extramarital sex destroys a marriage because it allows an artificial split between the good and the bad—the good is projected on the new partner and the bad is dumped on the head of the old. Dishonesty, hiding and cheating create walls between men and women. Infidelity is just a symp-

tom of trouble. It is a symbolic complaint, a weapon of revenge, as well as an unraveler of closeness. Infidelity is often that proverbial last straw that sinks the camel to the ground.

14   All right—marriage has always been difficult. Why then are we seeing so many divorces at this time? Yes, our modern social fabric is thin, and yes the permissiveness of society has created unrealistic expectations and thrown the family into chaos. But divorce is so common because people today are unwilling to exercise the self-discipline that marriage requires. They expect easy joy, like the entertainment on TV, the thrill of a good party.

15   Marriage takes some kind of sacrifice, not dreadful self-sacrifice of the soul, but some level of compromise. Some of one's fantasies, some of one's legitimate desires have to be given up for the value of the marriage itself. "While all marital partners feel shackled at times, it is they who really choose to make the marital ties into confining chains or supporting bonds," says Dr. Whitaker. Marriage requires sexual, financial and emotional discipline. A man and a woman cannot follow every impulse, cannot allow themselves to stop growing or changing.

16   Divorce is not an evil act. Sometimes it provides salvation for people who have grown hopelessly apart or were frozen in patterns of pain or mutual unhappiness. Divorce can be, despite its initial devastation, like the first cut of the surgeon's knife, a step toward new health and a good life. On the other hand, if the partners can stay past the breaking up of the romantic myths into the development of real love and intimacy, they have achieved a work as amazing as the greatest cathedrals of the world. Marriages that do not fail but improve, that persist despite imperfections, are not only rare these days but offer a wondrous shelter in which the face of our mutual humanity can safely show itself.

Exercise 3   Discussion and Critical Thinking

1. What is the subject (a situation, circumstance, or trend) at the center of this discussion?

2. Is this essay concerned more with causes, effects, or a combination?

3. What internal and external factors cause marriages to fail?

4. If it is true that we select marriage partners with qualities that will enable us to re-create our childhood experiences, both good and bad, then are those of us who had mostly bad childhood experiences trapped into reproducing those bad patterns?

5. According to Roiphe, what specific realities puncture the dreams of romantic love (paragraph 7)?

6. What are the components of (and thus the causes of) a good marriage?

The Story of an Hour

Kate Chopin

> *The author of this famous story on love and marriage, Kate Chopin, was left a widow with six children at age thirty-two. Turning to writing seriously, she wrote stories set mainly in the Creole bayou country around New Orleans. Her independent thinking, especially about women's emotions, attracted a firestorm of critical attention to her novel* The Awakening *and two collections of short stories,* Bayou Folk *and* A Night in Acadie, *and established her reputation as a feminist.*

1   Knowing that Mrs. Mallard was afflicted with a heart trouble, great care was taken to break to her as gently as possible the news of her husband's death.

2   It was her sister Josephine who told her, in broken sentences, veiled hints that revealed in half concealing. Her husband's friend Richards was there, too, near her. It was he who had been in the newspaper office when intelligence of the railroad disaster was received, with Brently Mallard's name leading the list of "killed." He had only taken the time to assure himself of its truth by a second telegram, and had hastened to forestall any less careful, less tender friend in bearing the sad message.

3   She did not hear the story as many women have heard the same, with a paralyzed inability to accept its significance. She wept at once, with sudden, wild abandonment, in her sister's arms. When the storm of grief had spent itself she went to her room alone. She would have no one follow her.

4   There stood, facing the open window, a comfortable, roomy armchair. Into this she sank, pressed down by a physical exhaustion that haunted her body and seemed to reach into her soul.

5   She could see in the open square before her house the tops of trees that were all aquiver with the new spring life. The delicious breath of rain was in the air. In the street below a peddler was crying his wares. The notes of a distant song which someone was singing reached her faintly, and countless sparrows were twittering in the eaves.

6   There were patches of blue sky showing here and there through the clouds that had met and piled one above the other in the west facing her window.

7   She sat with her head thrown back upon the cushion of the chair quite motionless, except when a sob came up into her throat and shook her, as a child who has cried itself to sleep continues to sob in its dreams.

8   She was young, with a fair, calm face, whose lines bespoke repression and even a certain strength. But now there was a dull stare in her eyes, whose gaze was fixed away off yonder on one of those patches of blue sky. It was not a glance of reflection, but rather indicated a suspension of intelligent thought.

9   There was something coming to her and she was waiting for it, fearfully. What was it? She did not know; it was too subtle and elusive to name. But she felt it, creeping out of the sky, reaching toward her through the sounds, the scents, the color that filled the air.

10   Now her bosom rose and fell tumultuously. She was beginning to recognize this thing that was approaching to possess her, and she was striving to beat it back with her will—as powerless as her two white slender hands would have been.

11   When she abandoned herself, a little whispered word escaped her slightly parted lips. She said it over and over under her breath: "Free, free, free!" The vacant stare and the look of terror that had followed it went from her eyes. They stayed keen and bright. Her pulses beat fast, and the coursing blood warmed and relaxed every inch of her body.

12   She did not stop to ask if it were not a monstrous joy that held her. A clear and exalted perception enabled her to dismiss the suggestion as trivial.

13   She knew that she would weep again when she saw the kind, tender hands folded in death; the face that had never

looked save with love upon her, fixed and gray and dead. But she saw beyond that bitter moment a long procession of years to come that would belong to her absolutely. And she opened and spread her arms out to them in welcome.

14   There would be no one to live for during those coming years; she would live for herself. There would be no powerful will bending her in that blind persistence with which men and women believe they have a right to impose a private will upon a fellow-creature. A kind intention or a cruel intention made the act seem no less a crime as she looked upon it in that brief moment of illumination.

15   And yet she had loved him—sometimes. Often she had not. What did it matter! What could love, the unsolved mystery, count for in face of this possession of self-assertion which she suddenly recognized as the strongest impulse of her being!

16   "Free! Body and soul free!" she kept whispering.

17   Josephine was kneeling before the closed door with her lips to the keyhole, imploring for admission. "Louise, open the door! I beg; open the door—you will make yourself ill. What are you doing, Louise? For heaven's sake open the door."

18   "Go away. I am not making myself ill." No; she was drinking in a very elixir of life through that open window.

19   Her fancy was running riot along those days ahead of her. Spring days, and summer days, and all sorts of days that would be her own. She breathed a quick prayer that life might be long. It was only yesterday she had thought with a shudder that life might be long.

20   She arose at length and opened the door to her sister's importunities. There was a feverish triumph in her eyes, and she carried herself unwittingly like a goddess of Victory. She clasped her sister's waist, and together they descended the stairs. Richards stood waiting for them at the bottom.

21   Some one was opening the door with a latchkey. It was Brently Mallard who entered, a little travel-stained, composedly carrying his grip-sack and umbrella. He had been far from the scene of the accident, and did not even know there had been one. He stood amazed at Josephine's piercing cry; at Richards's quick motion to screen him from the view of his wife.

22   But Richards was too late.

23   When the doctors came they said she had died of heart disease—of joy that kills.

Exercise 4   Discussion and Critical Thinking

1. What is Mrs. Mallard's first reaction on hearing of her husband's death?

2. What is her second reaction?

3. Why hasn't she considered freedom before?

4. Did her husband love her? Did she love him?

5. Did he abuse her?

6. Is this story mainly about women's rights, freedom, or some other subject?

7. Why does Mrs. Mallard die?

The Ballad of Anna Banana

John Cordell

> *This folk song from* Oklahoma, My Sweet Sorrow: Ballads as Memoirs *can be sung to the melody of "My Darlin' Clementine."*

Chorus:
Anna Banana, Anna Banana,
Anna Banana was her name,
She was the local weirdo,
And she brought her family shame.

She was dirty, she was smelly, in her farmer's overalls,
She'd stop and use the bushes to answer nature's calls.

Her nose was red and it was runny, her squinty eyes were crossed,
Her hair was long and matted, her upper teeth were lost.

When us boys would tease her, she'd laugh and slap her sides,
She was always left for walkin', no one would give her rides.

On the road one day she passed me, and I saw her drop some mail,
I hollered out to tell her, as she veered off on a trail.

When she didn't hear me, I thought I'd have some fun,
I'd read old Anna's letter, I'd take the words and run.

Chorus

I settled by a shade tree, I opened up her mail,
It was written by her husband, he was doin' time in jail.

I was startin' with my laughter, as I read his penciled scrawls,
He said he sent his love from beyond the prison walls.

He said that in his dreams he could feel her by his side,
He promised to come home and walk by her with pride.

He went on to get all mushy in scratches crude and strong,
For her he had some phrases he had borrowed from a song.

"Have I told you lately that I love you?
Could I tell you once again somehow?
Have I told you lately that I love you?
Well, darlin', I'm tellin' you now."*

Then my laughter got all chokey, and I gave up my plan,
I went chasin' after Anna, with that letter in my hand.

She still looked and smelled so awful, but I had a new concern,
If a man could love old Anna, I had much more to learn.

Chorus

Exercise 5 ┃ Discussion and Critical Thinking

1. About how old do you think the young narrator to be? Why? Is the ballad about mainly the narrator or Anna?

2. Why does it not occur to the narrator that Anna Banana might love and be loved?

---

*From the country song "Have I Told You Lately That I Love You?"

3. The narrator says he has much more to learn. What has he learned at the end of the ballad?

4. How would you characterize the love of Anna's husband for her? If you like, use a formula from "How Do I Love Thee?"

5. Do you think it would be more difficult or easier to love someone such as Anna Banana than someone such as _____ (a physically attractive celebrity)? Explain.

✳ Reading-Related Writing

"How Do I Love Thee?"

1. Write an essay about a love you are familiar with that can be defined by one of the eight variations in Sternberg's system.
2. Compare and contrast (see page 24 for techniques) two loves you are familiar with, according to definitions within Sternberg's system.

"Romantic Love, Courtship, and Marriage"

3. Write an essay in which you relate all or most of the six "characteristics that seem to attract people to one another" to a marriage or a relationship you are familiar with. Your example may support Robertson's views, or it may show that a marriage can be very good even though the partners do not share several of the six characteristics. (See Analysis by Division, page 18, and Cause and Effect, page 21.)
4. Write about a marriage that failed because the partners were too different, that is, they shared few or none of the six characteristics. (See Comparison and Contrast, page 24, and Cause and Effect, page 21.)
5. Write an essay in which you argue that the assets that prospective mates try to "sell" each other on (appearance, charm, common interests, career prospects) either are or are not more important than the six characteristics that attract people to each other. Use references to the article as well as your own examples. (See Analysis by Division, page 18, and Exemplification, page 18.)

6. Write an essay in which you rank the six "characteristics that seem to attract people to one another" and explain the reason for your ranking. (See Analysis by Division, page 18, and Classification, page 23.)

7. Discuss to what extent the six characteristics apply to same-sex relationships.

8. Robertson says that individuals in the "marriage market" try to sell themselves on the basis of "physical appearance, personal charms, talents and interests, and career prospects." Are those assets more important in mate selection than the six characteristics? Or are the assets merely complementary, just factors that go with the characteristics? Explain your conclusion and evaluate the relationship between assets and characteristics in an essay.

"Why Marriages Fail"

9. Explain the effects of a divorce on a person you know, either the child of divorced parents or a partner in a divorce. Consider both the immediate and the long-range effects. Keep in mind that Roiphe maintains that divorce is not necessarily a bad idea. (See Cause and Effect, page 21.)

10. Roiphe says that "we all select with unconscious accuracy a mate who will recreate with us the emotional patterns of our first homes." Either agree or disagree with that statement and support your views by discussing the causal factors in a marriage you are familiar with. (See Argument, page 28.)

11. Discuss an ideal marriage (a particular one, if possible) and explain what made it that way (causes). Consider paragraphs 8 through 13 for ideas on what Roiphe believes makes a good marriage.

    Roiphe says, "People can overcome the habits and attitudes that developed in childhood." Write an essay in which you show that she is right, or one in which you point out the difficulties in overcoming those habits and attitudes. Use specific examples (page 18) and stress the causes and/or effects (page 21).

"The Story of an Hour"

12. Create a diary account of some of the experiences Mrs. Mallard went through in her marriage—experiences that made her long for freedom. (See Narration, page 15, and Cause and Effect, page 21.)

13. Pose as the husband and write a eulogy that he would deliver at his wife's funeral. Include examples of the love they shared. Through his words, have him reveal what type of husband he was. For instance, he may reveal himself as a well-intentioned yet controlling person, but he will not recognize himself as such. (See Exemplification, page 18, and Narration, page 15.)

14. Write an essay in which you argue that Mrs. Mallard's reaction is far more likely to be experienced by a woman than by a man; or argue against that view. (See Argument, page 28.)

15. Discuss the issue of whether, if the roles were reversed, Mr. Mallard could die of the same shock that killed Mrs. Mallard.

16. Assume that Mrs. Mallard has empty love and Mr. Mallard has companionate love (see "How Do I Love Thee?" page 31) and compare and contrast these two characters in relation to the story's theme. (See Comparison and Contrast, page 24.)

17. Explain Mrs. Mallard's thirst for freedom. What would she like to get away from and where would she like to go? Might Roiphe's essay "Why Marriages Fail" shed some light on Mrs. Mallard's situation? Is Sternberg's system (described in Trotter's "How Do I Love Thee?") useful in providing a framework for discussing the elements of love that concern Mrs. Mallard? (See Analysis by Division, page 18.)

"The Ballad of Anna Banana"

18. Write about the properties of the love personified in this ballad. You may have to make some assumptions about the lives of Anna and her husband. Consider using terms from Sternberg's system (in Trotter's "How Do I Love Thee?") as a framework. (See Analysis by Division, page 18.)

19. Discuss the assumptions held and then reexamined by the narrator (the young child).

20. Write about an event or experience that inspired you to reexamine beliefs. This might also pertain to love, but it could relate to other ideas and definitions such as courage, family, self-sacrifice, self-reliance, patriotism, and heroism. (See Cause and Effect, page 21, and Definition, page 26.)

21. Write about the idea that the ballad is more about the narrator than Anna.

4

Your Cheatin' Heart

If you're a Snow Goose, you will mate for life and be faithful to your partner. If you're an American human being, chances are more than 20 percent that you will stray from the nest and about 50 percent that you will leave the nest. Moreover, another study reports that 98 percent of males and 80 percent of females confessed sexual fantasies about someone other than their partner. Snow Geese beaks are sealed on that topic.

Three readings explore the causes and effects of Americans' fantasies and affairs:

- "The Roots of Temptation" analyzes causes of cheating in imagination and reality.
- "The Girls in Their Summer Dresses" shows the cumulative effects of a wandering eye.
- "Frankie and Johnny" relates dire, graphic consequences of a cheatin' heart found out.

The Roots of Temptation

Benedict Carey

> *In this article,* Los Angeles Times *staff writer Benedict Carey reviews contemporary psychological and sociological studies of sexual unfaithfulness between couples.*

1   A simple plea for reassurance—*You'd tell me, wouldn't you?*—is about all the discussion many couples can manage on the topic of marital infidelity. It's rarely a genuine request: Everyone knows it could happen, but very few of us would really want to know that it did. The topic of infidelity is off limits for most couples. . . .

2   For many years, most of what scientists knew about infidelity came from marital therapists' interviews with clients or from psychologists who asked men and women to answer questions about hypothetical affairs. In the last few years, however,

50

researchers have finally begun to conduct larger, more rigorous surveys, asking about real experiences. The evidence has contributed to an emerging body of thinking about who cheats, when and why.

3   Contrary to one commonly held view, many people who report being in happy marriages commit adultery. Their yearning for variety warps their judgment, even when they fully appreciate the risks of infidelity. For when an affair is revealed, clinicians report, the impact on the marriage is usually catastrophic. . . .

Taking a Closer Look

4   The prevalence of infidelity is coming into sharper focus. Several recent surveys suggest that the majority of people do not cheat, either because they cannot bear the thought of betrayal, cannot drum up the interest or perhaps have already known the profound pain of losing an important relationship. Yet the studies find that more than one in five Americans do have an affair, at least once in their lives, and that women are now about as likely as men to cross the line.

5   The first few years of marriage are clearly a red zone, new research shows. An analysis conducted in 2000 by sociologists in New York found two distinct patterns in the timing of affairs. A married woman's likelihood of straying is highest in the first five years, and falls off gradually with time, according to the survey of 3,432 U.S. adults. Men have two high-risk phases, one during the first five years of marriage and again, after the 20th year.

6   The psychological underpinnings of early affairs often are tied up with the vows themselves, some experts believe. As well-intentioned as they can be, vows are still open-ended pledges—of unknown cost, of blind sacrifice. Very often, their gravity doesn't sink in right away; and young married men and women often have a lingering appetite for the flirtation and sexually charged attention that was the lifeblood of their single lives, marital therapists say.

7   Newlyweds' expectations of wedded bliss can set them up for profound disappointment, after the florists and caterers are gone and the reality of living with a spouse becomes clear. And if there are no children on the way, to deepen and broaden the character of the bond, the yearning for variety and attention outside the marriage often still runs very high, psychologists find.

8   "One reason for starting an affair, especially for young couples, is rebelliousness against the vows, against the very idea that 'I'm never ever going to make love to another person,'" said Joel Block, a clinical psychologist in New York and author of *Naked Intimacy* (McGraw Hill, 2003).

9   Even when people welcome the sacrifice, and honor vows without reservation, the promises can lend a false sense of security. The commitment is firm, but the imagination may lag behind. In one recent study, University of Vermont psychologists surveyed 180 couples who were either married or living with a partner. Fully 98% of males and 80% of females reported having a sexual fantasy about someone other than their partner, at least once in the previous two months. The longer couples were together, the more likely both partners were to report having fantasies; but the imagined flings were still very common in young married couples, who often assumed that they should be immune.

10   In short, almost everyone is doing it—at least in their heads.

11   And usually they can't talk about it, especially with the person closest to them. This creates one of the universal paradoxes of romantic desire, a tension between public faithfulness and private longing for another, a secret life of the imagination.

12   Some married people can live with this paradox and understand it as an entirely internal drama that in no way presages a real affair or reflects any need to stray. Yet even long-married people who are acutely aware of this double life and can joke with themselves about it aren't always able to resolve their tension. In a psychological sense, free-floating desire has provided the brain with an idea of infidelity, complete with expectations, curiosities and what-ifs. The frequency and vividness of these thoughts may themselves lead a man or woman to believe their love for a partner is fading.

13   Then something happens. A blowout argument. A promotion. A school reunion, the loss of a job, an e-mail from an old boyfriend. Some triumph or loss that opens a door through which a person is now primed to walk. The delights of an affair have already been richly imagined. The consequences are now minimized: "Many couples survive affairs; stop depriving yourself; it's an experience, part of the richness of life," a person might tell herself or himself.

14   "Whatever the final provocation," [one observer] said, "the person decides—actively makes a choice to participate at every step along the way."

15   The evidence that this kind of logic can lead people astray from apparently satisfying, long-lived, stable relationships is circumstantial but compelling. In one recent analysis, researchers at UC Irvine found that people who claimed their marriage was "very happy" were two times as likely to cheat on their spouses as those who said their marriage was "extremely happy."

What Drives Them?

16   The given reasons for these affairs range widely. In research for a book, Diane Shader Smith, a Los Angeles writer, has conducted in-depth interviews with more than 175 married women who have had or were currently involved in an affair. There were "revenge" flings: One woman had a brief affair after she found out that her (now former) husband had cheated on her. There were "motivational" flings: An L.A. doctor's wife has had affairs whenever she needs some impetus to lose weight. And certainly love can come into play: One middle-aged woman living out in the country had a 10-year affair with her neighbor's husband.

17   "One thing many had in common was chemistry," Smith said. "They all described that, the chemistry with another man, the casual brush against the arm, that orgasm-on-the-spot feeling," she said. Most of the women interviewed were unapologetic, Smith said; many had kept their secret, and preferred to stay in their marriage, risks and all. In previous surveys, men have expressed similar motives, although primarily focused on the thrill of sensual pleasure.

18   Psychologists may never know the true impact of infidelity on marriage. Most couples do not seek therapy, whether an affair is suspected or revealed. Among couples who do pursue counseling, however, there's little doubt: Infidelity hits like Hurricane Isabel.

19   In one recent study of 62 Israeli couples seeing therapists to help cope with their affairs, a third eventually divorced; about half limped along in still-troubled marriages, according to researchers at Hebrew University, in Jerusalem. Only nine of the couples, or 14%, seemed to bounce back and show signs of real growth and optimism in their marriage, the psychologists reported.

Traveling a Rocky Road

20   Several recent studies have tracked how men and women react when a partner's affair is revealed. The pattern is familiar: emotional chaos, which can last for months; then reflection and self-questioning, which can go on even longer; and finally, a decision whether to forgive, if not forget.

21   In one ongoing study, researchers at UCLA and the University of Washington in Seattle have been tracking 134 couples in marriages deemed "very troubled" as they attend weekly therapy sessions. Those couples whose relationships were most damaged, by psychological measures, tended to be the same ones who were reeling from affairs, said David Atkins, of the Fuller Theological Seminary. Yet after six months of therapy, these 19 couples had made greater gains in repairing their relationships than the others. In part, that's because they started at the bottom, he said. But there also appeared to be something else at work.

22   "These couples were very unhappy at the start, but they also had shown heroic perseverance in the face of this betrayal," Atkins said. "In no way do we want to say that infidelity is good. But it may be that, at least for these couples, the affair gave them one huge major issue to focus on in the therapy."

Exercise 1 Discussion and Critical Thinking

1. One study showed that 98 percent of males and 80 percent of females had had sexual fantasies about someone other than their partner during the previous two months. How would you account for that difference?

2. Carey says that "almost everyone is doing it—at least in their heads. And usually they can't talk about it, especially with the person closest to them." Would it be helpful in most cases if people were more open and honest with everyone, including their partners?

3. Of the three reasons for women having affairs, as discussed in the article—revenge, motivation, and love (just chemistry in the shorter term)—which do you think is the leading cause?

4. What is the final impact of discovered affairs on most relationships?

5. The last two paragraphs discuss nineteen very troubled marriages in which the couples were dealing with affairs. Why were those couples able to make progress?

The Girls in Their Summer Dresses

Irwin Shaw

> *Michael looks at the girls, and his wife, Frances, becomes annoyed. Is Irwin Shaw writing only about two individuals in this short story, or do the characters represent a general, and long-standing, division between the sexes?*

1   Fifth Avenue was shining in the sun when they left the Brevoort. The sun was warm, even though it was February, and everything looked like Sunday morning—the buses and the well-dressed people walking slowly in couples and the quiet buildings with the windows closed.

2   Michael held Frances' arm tightly as they walked toward Washington Square in the sunlight. They walked lightly, almost smiling, because they had slept late and had a good breakfast and it was Sunday. Michael unbuttoned his coat and let it flap around him in the mild wind.

3   "Look out," Frances said as they crossed Eighth Street. "You'll break your neck."

4   Michael laughed and Frances laughed with him.

5   "She's not so pretty," Frances said. "Anyway, not pretty enough to take a chance of breaking your neck."

6   Michael laughed again. "How did you know I was looking at her?"

7   Frances cocked her head to one side and smiled at her husband under the brim of her hat. "Mike, darling," she said.

8   "O.K.," he said. "Excuse me."

9   Frances patted his arm lightly and pulled him along a little faster toward Washington Square. "Let's not see anybody all day," she said. "Let's just hang around with each other. You and me. We're always up to our neck in people, drinking their Scotch or drinking our Scotch; we only see each other in bed. I want to go out with my husband all day long. I want him to talk only to me and listen only to me."

10   "What's to stop us?" Michael asked.

11   "The Stevensons. They want us to drop by around one o'clock and they'll drive us into the country."

12   "The cunning Stevensons," Mike said. "Transparent. They can whistle. They can go driving in the country by themselves."

13   "Is it a date?"

14   "It's a date."

15   Frances leaned over and kissed him on the tip of the ear.

16   "Darling," Michael said, "this is Fifth Avenue."

17   "Let me arrange a program," Frances said. "A planned Sunday in New York for a young couple with money to throw away."

18   "Go easy."

19   "First let's go to the Metropolitan Museum of Art," Frances suggested, because Michael had said during the week he wanted to go. "I haven't been there in three years and there're at least ten pictures I want to see again. Then we can take the bus down to Radio City and watch them skate. And later we'll go down to Cavanaugh's and get a steak as big as a blacksmith's apron, with a bottle of wine, and after that there's a French picture at the Filmarte that everybody says—say, are you listening to me?"

20   "Sure," he said. He took his eyes off the hatless girl with the dark hair, cut dancer-style like a helmet, who was walking past him.

21   "That's the program for the day," Frances said flatly. "Or maybe you'd just rather walk up and down Fifth Avenue."

22   "No," Michael said. "Not at all."

23   "You always look at other women," Frances said. "Everywhere. Every damned place we go."

24   "No, darling," Michael said, "I look at everything. God gave me eyes and I look at women and men and subway excavations and moving pictures and the little flowers of the field. I casually inspect the universe."

25   "You ought to see the look in your eye," Frances said, "as you casually inspect the universe on Fifth Avenue."

26   "I'm a happily married man." Michael pressed her elbow tenderly. "Example for the whole twentieth century—Mr. and Mrs. Mike Loomis. Hey, let's have a drink," he said, stopping.

27   "We just had breakfast."

28   "Now listen, darling," Mike said, choosing his words with care, "it's a nice day and we both felt good and there's no reason why we have to break it up. Let's have a nice Sunday."

29   "All right. I don't know why I started this. Let's drop it. Let's have a good time."

30   They joined hands consciously and walked without talking among the baby carriages and the old Italian men in their Sunday clothes and the young women with Scotties in Washington Square Park.

31   "At least once a year everyone should go to the Metropolitan Museum of Art," Frances said after a while, her tone a good imitation of the tone she had used at breakfast and at the beginning of their walk. "And it's nice on Sunday. There're a lot of people looking at the pictures and you get the feeling maybe Art isn't on the decline in New York City, after all—"

32   "I want to tell you something," Michael said very seriously. "I have not touched another woman. Not once. In all the five years."

33   "All right," Frances said.

34   "You believe that, don't you?"

35   "All right."

36   They walked between the crowded benches, under the scrubby city-park trees.

37   "I try not to notice it," Frances said, "but I feel rotten inside, in my stomach, when we pass a woman and you look at her and I see that look in your eye and that's the way you looked at me the first time. In Alice Maxwell's house. Standing there in the living room, next to the radio, with a green hat on and all those people."

38   "I remember the hat," Michael said.

39   "The same look," Frances said. "And it makes me feel bad. It makes me feel terrible."

40   "Sh-h-h, please, darling, sh-h-h."

41   "I think I would like a drink now," Frances said.

42   They walked over to a bar on Eighth Street, not saying anything, Michael automatically helping her over curbstones and guiding her past automobiles. They sat near a window in the bar and the sun streamed in and there was a small, cheerful fire in the fireplace. A little Japanese waiter came over and put down some pretzels and smiled happily at them.

43   "What do you order after breakfast?" Michael asked.

44   "Brandy, I suppose," Frances said.

45   "Courvoisier," Michael told the waiter. "Two Courvoisiers."

46   The waiter came with the glasses and they sat drinking the brandy in the sunlight. Michael finished half his and drank a little water.

47   "I look at women," he said. "Correct. I don't say it's wrong
or right. I look at them. If I pass them on the street and I don't
look at them, I'm fooling you, I'm fooling myself."

48   "You look at them as though you want them," Frances said,
playing with her brandy glass. "Every one of them."

49   "In a way," Michael said, speaking softly and not to his
wife, "in a way that's true. I don't do anything about it, but it's
true."

50   "I know it. That's why I feel bad."

51   "Another brandy," Michael called. "Waiter, two more
brandies."

52   He sighed and closed his eyes and rubbed them gently with
his fingertips. "I love the way women look. One of the things
I like best about New York is the battalions of women. When I
first came to New York from Ohio that was the first thing I no-
ticed, the million wonderful women, all over the city. I walked
around with my heart in my throat."

53   "A kid," Frances said. "That's a kid's feeling."

54   "Guess again," Michael said. "Guess again. I'm older now.
I'm a man getting near middle age, putting on a little fat and I
still love to walk along Fifth Avenue at three o'clock on the east
side of the street between Fiftieth and Fifty-seventh Streets.
They're all out then, shopping, in their furs and their crazy hats,
everything all concentrated from all over the world into seven
blocks—the best furs, the best clothes, the handsomest women,
out to spend money and feeling good about it."

55   The Japanese waiter put the two drinks down, smiling with
great happiness.

56   "Everything is all right?" he asked.

57   "Everything is wonderful," Michael said.

58   "If it's just a couple of fur coats," Frances said, "and forty-
five-dollar hats—"

59   "It's not the fur coats. Or the hats. That's just the scenery
for that particular kind of woman. Understand," he said, "you
don't have to listen to this."

60   "I want to listen."

61   "I like the girls in the offices. Neat, with their eyeglasses,
smart, chipper, knowing what everything is about. I like the
girls on Forty-fourth Street at lunchtime, the actresses, all
dressed up on nothing a week. I like the salesgirls in the stores,
paying attention to you first because you're a man, leaving lady
customers waiting. I got all this stuff accumulated in me be-

cause I've been thinking about it for ten years and now you've asked for it and here it is."

62   "Go ahead," Frances said.

63   "When I think of New York City, I think of all the girls on parade in the city. I don't know whether it's something special with me or whether every man in the city walks around with the same feeling inside him, but I feel as though I'm at a picnic in this city. I like to sit near the women in the theatres, the famous beauties who've taken six hours to get ready and look it. And the young girls at the football games, with the red cheeks, and when the warm weather comes, the girls in their summer dresses." He finished his drink. "That's the story."

64   Frances finished her drink and swallowed two or three times extra. "You say you love me?"

65   "I love you."

66   "I'm pretty, too," Frances said. "As pretty as any of them."

67   "You're beautiful," Michael said.

68   "I'm good for you," Frances said, pleading. "I've made a good wife, a good housekeeper, a good friend. I'd do any damn thing for you."

69   "I know," Michael said. He put his hand out and grasped hers.

70   "You'd like to be free to—" Frances said.

71   "Sh-h-h."

72   "Tell the truth." She took her hand away from under his.

73   Michael flicked the edge of his glass with his finger. "O.K," he said gently. "Sometimes I feel I would like to be free."

74   "Well," Frances said, "any time you say."

75   "Don't be foolish." Michael swung his chair around to her side of the table and patted her thigh.

76   She began to cry silently into her handkerchief, bent over just enough so nobody else in the bar would notice. "Someday," she said, crying, "you're going to make a move."

77   Michael didn't say anything. He sat watching the bartender slowly peel a lemon.

78   "Aren't you?" Frances asked harshly. "Come on, tell me. Talk. Aren't you?"

79   "Maybe," Michael said. He moved his chair back again. "How the hell do I know?"

80   "You know," Frances persisted. "Don't you know?"

81   "Yes," Michael said after a while, "I know."

82   Frances stopped crying then. Two or three snuffles into the

handkerchief and she put it away and her face didn't tell anything to anybody. "At least do me a favor," she said.

83   "Sure."

84   "Stop talking about how pretty this woman is or that one. Nice eyes, nice breasts, a pretty figure, good voice." She mimicked his voice. "Keep it to yourself. I'm not interested."

85   Michael waved to the waiter. "I'll keep it to myself," he said.

86   Frances flicked the corners of her eyes. "Another brandy," she told the waiter.

87   "Two," Michael said.

88   "Yes, Ma'am; yes, Sir," said the waiter, backing away.

89   Frances regarded Michael coolly cross the table. "Do you want me to call the Stevensons?" she asked. "It'll be nice in the country."

90   "Sure," Michael said. "Call them."

91   She got up from the table and walked across the room toward the telephone. Michael watched her walk, thinking what a pretty girl, what nice legs.

Exercise 2   Discussion and Critical Thinking

1. Is this story mainly about causes or effects of temptation?

2. How important are the surroundings to Michael's unfaithfulness of the mind?

3. Would Michael be less tempted if he were to stay away from places such as Fifth Avenue and "girls in their summer dresses"?

4. Would Frances rest more easily if she were to read "The Roots of Temptation" in this book?

5. How does the behavior of both characters change after Michael starts looking at other women?

6. Who is more at fault, Frances or Michael? Explain.

7. What is the significance of Michael's last observation of Frances?

8. What do you think will happen to their marriage? Why?

9. What is your opinion of the argument that men and women are different—that women want monogamy and men want polygamy? How would that argument apply to this short story and to the essay "The Roots of Temptation"?

10. What would be your advice to Frances and Michael?

Frankie and Johnny

Anonymous

> *Frankie really loved the guy, but he "was doin' her wrong." She shot him dead. This ballad narrates the whole story of one of the best-known crimes of passion in folk literature. For guitar chord arrangements use the Google search engine and key in "Frankie and Johnny guitar chords."*

Frankie and Johnny were lovers,
Oh Lordy, how they could love.
They swore to be true to each other,
True as the stars above,
5 He was her man, but he was doin' her wrong.

Frankie she was a good woman
As everybody knows,
Spent a hundred dollars
Just to buy her man some clothes.
10 He was her man, but he was doing her wrong.

Frankie went down to the corner
Just for a bucket of beer,
She said, "Mr. Bartender,
Has my loving Johnny been here?
15 He was my man, but he's a-doing me wrong."

"Now I don't want to tell you no stories
And I don't want to tell you no lies
I saw your man about an hour ago
With a gal named Nellie Bligh
20 He was your man, but he's a-doing you wrong."

Frankie went down to the hotel
Didn't go there for fun,
Underneath her kimona
She carried a forty-four gun.
25 He was her man, but he was doing her wrong.

Frankie looked over the transom
To see what she could spy,
There sat Johnny on the sofa
Just loving up Nellie Bligh.
30 He was her man, but he was doing her wrong.

Frankie got off that ladder
She didn't want to see no more;
Rooty-toot-toot three times she did shoot
Right through that hardwood door.
35 He was her man, but he was doing her wrong.

Now the first time Frankie shot Johnny
He let out an awful yell,
The second time she shot him
There was a new man's face in hell.
40 He was her man, but he was doing her wrong.

"Oh, roll me over easy
Roll me over slow
Roll me over on the right side
For the left side hurts me so."
45 He was her man, but he was doing her wrong.

Sixteen rubber-tired carriages
Sixteen rubber-tired hacks
They take poor Johnny to the graveyard
They ain't gonna bring him back.
50 He was her man, but he was doing her wrong.

Frankie looked out of the jailhouse
To see what she could see,
All she could hear was a two-string bow
Crying, "Nearer my God to thee."
55 He was her man, but he was doing her wrong.

Frankie she said to the sheriff,
"What do you reckon they'll do?"
The sheriff he said to Frankie,
"It's the electric chair for you."
60 He was her man, but he was doing her wrong.

This story has no moral
This story has no end
This story only goes to show
That there ain't no good in men!
65 He was her man, but he was doing her wrong.

Exercise 3 Discussion and Critical Thinking

1. As a ballad, this is a narrative (see page 15). Fill in the parts:

    Situation:

    Conflict:

    Struggle:

    Result:

    Meaning:

2. The song says, "There ain't no good in men." Reading (or
   singing) these words and reflecting on what you have read in
   "The Roots of Temptation" may lead you to a different
   conclusion. If so, what is it?

3. If Frankie had come to you before she loaded her .44, what
   would you have told her in simple, philosophical terms?

✳ Reading-Related Writing

"The Roots of Temptation"

1. Write an essay about a situation you are familiar with in terms
   of generalizations on matters such as temptation, fantasies, and
   cheating discussed by Carey. You might write about a relation-

ship that failed or deteriorated because of cheating or even about one that was eventually strengthened because of the way a couple dealt with infidelity. (See Narration, page 15, and Cause and Effect, page 21.)

2. Carey discusses three reasons for cheating—revenge, motivation, and chemistry. Write an essay in which you discuss all three causes (see Cause and Effect, page 21, and Classification, page 23), perhaps ranking them. Base your explanation on your independent insights, as well as on what you have learned from reading the essay.

"The Girls in Their Summer Dresses"

3. Write a comparison-and-contrast essay about Michael and Frances. Use particular moments in their conversation (such as at the beginning, then when she becomes annoyed, when they decide to have a drink, and when they decide to visit with friends) or character traits (such as honesty, loyalty, love, affection, lust, forgiveness) for points in your organization. (See Comparison and Contrast, page 24.)

4. Analyze Frances or Michael, using character traits such as those indicated in question 3. (See Analysis by Division, page 18.)

5. State the theme (meaning) that you think the author implies, and then agree or disagree with it.

6. Write a narrative in which you show how the characters' behavior becomes more self-conscious, mechanical, and detached as the story progresses. (See Narration, page 15.)

7. Develop a persuasive essay in which you argue that either Michael or Frances is primarily at fault. (See Argument, page 28.)

8. Argue that neither Michael nor Frances is at fault because men and women simply have different views toward male-female relationships. (See Comparison and Contrast, page 24, and Argument, page 28.)

9. Imagine the couple a year or so in the future, and write about them at that time. (See Narration, page 15.)

"Frankie and Johnny"

10. Retell this song as a short story. Think of a simple narrative account written in sentences with more details and more dialogue. Keep in mind that the book version is a folk ballad and that there are many versions. In one, Frankie is so appealing that the judge frees her and then marries her. Feel free to invent and alter details.

✳ 5

Drivers: Youngsters—Oldsters/ Speedsters—Slowsters

Try this hypothetical situation and question: You're driving on a two-lane highway and you see a car barreling toward you, riding the yellow line. Would you prefer the driver to be sixteen or seventy-six? It's not fair to say that you don't like those tricky *either-or* questions and that instead of choosing one driver or the other, you'd rather take a detour through a corn patch full of raging cape buffalo. Or perhaps you're more coolly analytical and would like to call a hypothetical-question timeout while you peruse relevant statistics on your cell phone or in-dash computer. Think it over.

Meanwhile, for immediate answers, casts a high beam on the two essays in this chapter:

- "Let Granny Drive If She Can" casts a qualified vote for old-sters.
- "A Modest Proposal, Guys Shouldn't Drive Till 25" proposes a national law for grounding drivers of a specific gender and age.

Let Granny Drive If She Can

Suzanne Fields

> *A syndicated columnist for the* Washington Times, *Suzanne Fields writes opinion articles twice a week on topics that often polarize her readers. Here she addresses the idea of restricting drivers' privileges because of age.*

1   My mother at 85 was alert, with good vision and sharp re-flexes for her age, but one day she smashed into three parked cars on a supermarket parking lot. We never found out exactly how it happened—she was not sure, either—but the investigators figured Mom hit the accelerator instead of the brake. When the car didn't slow down, she panicked and pushed down harder on the wrong pedal. This may be what happened to the 86-year-old man who plowed through that California farmers' market.

2   Mom was lucky, even though she spent two weeks in the hospital with two broken ribs. But we reluctantly concluded that it was time to take Mom's car keys. This was the hardest thing I have ever had to do. She pleaded, cajoled and demanded to keep her car. I was "mean" and "unfeeling," and her gentle voice grew strident. Tears trickled down her cheeks. I think she never felt old until that moment, when I took away the independence provided by the car. I felt like the wicked witch of the west, and the other points of the compass as well.

3   In the days that followed, we suggested that she take taxis to visit friends and to shop, but she wouldn't do it: "That's not my style." A driver was out of the question because she had no set places she had to go. She was not a lady for "Driving Miss Daisy." Fortunately, she lived in the city and quickly slipped into the routine of taking the bus, which she hadn't done since high school. She got to know the bus drivers and waved at them as they drove past her on her frequent strolls through the neighborhood. She began to enjoy her new life. But most old people have no convenient public transportation or shops within walking distance.

4   Hard as it was on both of us, we made the right decision in Mom's case. But is tragedy like that in Santa Monica a reason to take away the car keys of the elderly? I think not. Unless we learn how to play God, foreseeing accidents, that's the wrong lesson to learn.

5   Age doesn't necessarily prove anything. Slower reflexes or not, senior citizens are much better drivers than, for example, teenagers. They usually drive more slowly. They get honked at a lot, but their slower speed reduces the risk of death and destruction that accompanies speeding tons of metal. The worst risk-takers on the highway are young men between the ages of 18 to 25, but no one suggests taking away their keys or raising the driving age to 26.

6   The fatality rate in 2001 for motorists between 16 and 20, according to the National Highway Traffic Safety Administration, was more than double that for drivers over 70. The AARP estimates that drivers 55 and older compose a quarter of the driving population, but have only 18 percent of the accidents. The older the driver, the fewer miles he puts on his car. As the baby boomers age, the numbers of older drivers will increase. Large majorities of them live in the suburbs or in the countryside without public transportation. Rural and suburban communities

must arrange for alternative kinds of transportation for those who are failing in their driving ability; demand can drive public and entrepreneurial innovation.

7   Preventive remedies for the aging driver abound. Their licenses could be renewed at shorter intervals, with tougher physical tests. At the first signs of diminished alertness, a designated adult in the family should monitor the elderly driver closely for the good of everyone else. They shouldn't drink and drive, but who should? Doctors who prescribe medications for the elderly must make them aware of their influence on driving.

8   The older citizen who tries to avoid danger is likely to take personal responsibility with considerably more seriousness than a younger person who courts danger through partying and risk. I like the example of Lord Renton, the 94-year-old "Father of the House of Lords" in London, who volunteered the other day to take his first driving test. He first drove a car in England before 1935, the year a driver's license was first required. He enjoyed a grandfather clause, you might say.

9   Deciding he owed it to himself and his fellow drivers to submit to a test, he submitted himself to the indignity of taking the test on a small and unfamiliar Ford sedan, not his usual cup of tea. He succeeded brilliantly. We could expect no less from seniors on this side of the Atlantic. So, let's let Granny drive for as long as she can. Road age is a lot less dangerous than road rage.

Exercise 1 Discussion and Critical Thinking

1. What two paragraphs state the author's proposition and summarize her support?

2. What two other patterns of writing (narration, exemplification, comparison and contrast, process analysis, analysis by division) does Fields use significantly to advance her argument?

3. List the several forms of evidence Fields uses.

4. Fields mentions that young men between the ages of 18 and 25 are the worst drivers, but no one suggests taking their licenses away because of age. Why does that view prevail?

5. What is your reaction to Fields's argument?

6. Fields personalizes her argument by discussing her mother's situation. What effect does that approach have on her overall presentation?

A Modest Proposal: Guys Shouldn't Drive Till 25

Joyce Gallagher

> *Freelance writer Joyce Gallagher says we should look at the national problem of motor vehicle accidents and take a "drastic" step. To Gallagher, statistics tell the story, and the solution is as inevitable to her as it may be unthinkable to you.*

1   In the year 2001, 57,480 people were killed in motor vehicle accidents. That figure is within a few hundred of being the same number as those killed in the Vietnam War. We took drastic measures back in the early 1970s and ended that war in a way shocking to some: we left. The time has come for another drastic scheme. We need to recognize the main causes of this highway carnage and take action. According to the U.S. Department of Transportation, 25.1 percent of the roadway fatalities involve an age group constituting only 14.5 percent of the driving public. That group is the age range from 15 to 25. Within that group, one half are males. They are three times more likely to be involved in roadway fatalities, meaning that the about 7 percent males are responsible for more than 18 percent of roadway fatalities. This proposal may be a hard sell for politicians, but it is time for us to step forward boldly and raise the legal driving age for males nationally to 25.

2   Some may protest that it is unfair to punish the good young male drivers for the sins of their irresponsible peers. But we're already discriminating by group. Surely we all agree that drivers of a certain age should not be allowed to drive. That age varies from state to state, but it is around 15 or 16. We have concluded that those younger than 15 are too immature. We don't say

those under 15 should be treated individually, not even on the basis of gender. Instead, we exclude the offending group. With my proposal, we would simply move the legal age of male drivers to 25, lumping those of similar age and sex together for the good of society.

3   For you who say that some oldsters are also menaces on the roadways, I would like to point out that those over 88 are equal only to those between 15 and 25 for being involved in fatal crashes. Moreover, the crashes by super-seniors are likely to be caused by physical and mental impairments, which can be detected by periodic tests and remedied by pulled licenses, whereas the young, often irresponsible and impatient, are more likely to be guided by thrill-seeking impulses, tantrums, and other byproducts of testosterone, all of which are hopelessly glandular.

4   Although one salient reason—that this group of young males is responsible for the deaths of so many fellow citizens—is enough support for the proposed law, there are many side benefits for society.

- While the male 15–25 age group is waiting to drive motor vehicles, they would have time to improve their cultural lives and to lay groundwork for better driving skills and improved mental and physical health.
- Many youngsters would customarily ride with statistically superior female or elder drivers and could learn from the relatively good examples they witness.
- Being no more dependent on driving almost everywhere, the male youngsters would walk more or ride bikes or skateboards, providing them wholesome exercise so often neglected in our paunchy, weight-challenged society.
- As a group they would also use more public transportation, relieving traffic congestion on our roadways and reducing congestion in the air we breathe.
- Support for public transportation projects would soar, and cars might cease to be near the center of our lives.
- Car payment money now impoverishing so many young males might go toward savings, education, home improvement, self-improvement, and family activities.
- Gratitude from young male drivers for the rides provided by female spouses and other loved ones could promote affectionate and appreciative relationships and diminish road rage.

5   The only exceptions to this new national law would be for

the military and for public security and emergency agencies. Within the armed services, male personnel under 25 would be allowed to drive on foreign soil or on military property at any time. Male drivers working for police, fire, rescue, and ambulance services would drive only when on duty and their permits would be terminated for any serious traffic infraction. No doubt, some male youngsters, obsessed with driving motor vehicles, would join our public service sectors, making our national security and infrastructural services stronger so we could all sleep more peacefully.

6   Probably some males would protest this law and would try to circumvent it with devious strategies. Such resistance could be easily combated. For example, those who attempt to cross-dress or dye their hair gray for the purpose of obtaining a drivers' license could be charged with a felony.

7   Several people who have read my modest proposal have suggested that young men are victims of their own bodies and should be granted a "testosterone dementia exemption." Then, they could take injections of estrogen to neutralize the male hormones raging like tiny bulls within their systems. However, even these critics would surely concede that there could be a feminizing reaction to estrogen, one both psychological and physiological. Because of the possible physical side effects, wives of young men might find estrogen therapy unacceptable. A youthful bride might willingly bear the burden of transporting her husband to work and back, but she would almost certainly recoil at the thought of his wearing her bra.

8   Some might argue that improved drivers' education programs in our school system, better public transportation, the production of vehicles that are no more powerful and threatening than they need be, a reduced speed limit, counseling and restrictions for repeat offenders, and a stricter enforcement of existing laws represent a wiser approach to our national problem. However, because those ideas have failed to resonate, and young males have continued to put the pedal to the metal in a flood of blood, it is time for a simple statement that will fit on your bumper sticker:

> ## Guys Shouldn't
> ## Drive Till 25

Exercise 2 Discussion and Critical Thinking

1. What is the proposition?

2. How is the proposition introduced in the first paragraph?

3. How is the proposition qualified?

4. Which paragraph covers the main rebuttal (addressing the main anticipated point(s) of the opposition)?

5. What is Gallagher's main support?

6. In what way are the bulleted items related to support?

7. Would this law create some problems not discussed by the author?

8. Which of the bulleted items would you disagree with and why?

9. Do you think the author is entirely serious about this argument? What author comments might suggest that she is not?

10. Does it make any difference that the author is female? Why or why not?

※ Reading-Related Writing

"Let Granny Drive If She Can"

1. Write an argument in which you disagree with Fields's views. Make it an independent statement or a critique of Fields's article. (See Argument, page 28.)

2. Write an argument in which you agree with Fields's views. Your argument should be either personalized with your own examples or presented as a more formal argument without personal examples. (See Argument, page 28.)

"A Modest Proposal: Guys Shouldn't Drive Till 25"

3. Evaluate Gallagher's argument. Does she exaggerate to make her point? Is she just being colorful in advancing a reasonable argument? Discuss her logic. Is her argument to be taken literally or is she saying something else indirectly? (See Analysis by Division, page 18.)

4. Write an argument in which you either agree or disagree with Gallagher's views. Make it an independent statement or a critique of specifically what she said. Consider using examples from your own experience. (See Argument, page 28.)

5. Write an argument in which you propose a plan to deal with troublesome old and young drivers. If you incorporate ideas from the two essays in this chapter, acknowledge the source(s). (See Argument, page 28.)

✳ 6

Neat—Freaks and Foes

Are you fundamentally orderly or disorderly? We all have tendencies toward one or the other extreme. Some of us are hardcore, to our shame or pride. If we lean toward the disorderly, we may scoff at the opposite, referring to them as "uptight" or "anal retentive." If we are in the orderly camp, we may pity the disorderly for failures in work ethic, analytical power, self-discipline, even personal hygiene.

As we read Suzanne Britt's essay, we are probably first surprised and then charmed by her wit and satirical jibes. She insists that the neat (orderly) people are the bad guys and that the sloppy (disorderly) people are the good guys. Moreover, to her, the distinction is not even close. She says, "Neat people are lazier and meaner than sloppy people." She doesn't use the slang term "neat freaks," but she makes it clear that the neat are twisted, self-centered individuals who "cut a clean swath through the organic as well as the inorganic world."

Joyce Gallagher, author of "The Messy Are in Denial," is one of those people whom she characterizes as the organized. Her group has a preordained mission—to save and sustain the less fortunate, the disorganized, the sloppy. A bemused and grudgingly forgiving participant (after all, the disorganized can't help themselves), she traces the history of the organized and disorganized from a recent yard sale back to cave dwellers, saying that human nature hasn't changed much. The disorganized flounder, often in endearing ways, and the organized come to their rescue because of a genetic imperative.

Neat People vs. Sloppy People

Suzanne Britt

> *In this essay from her book* Show and Tell, *Suzanne Britt discusses two kinds of people, the neat and the sloppy. Wouldn't the world be a better place if we were all a bit neater? If you think so, prepare to argue with Suzanne Britt.*

1   I've finally figured out the difference between neat people and sloppy people. The distinction is, as always, moral. Neat people are lazier and meaner than sloppy people.

2   Sloppy people, you see, are not really sloppy. Their sloppi-
ness is merely the unfortunate consequence of their extreme
moral rectitude. Sloppy people carry in their mind's eye a heav-
enly vision, a precise plan, that is so stupendous, so perfect, it
can't be achieved in this world or the next.

3   Sloppy people live in Never-Never Land. Someday is their
métier. Someday they are planning to alphabetize all their
books and set up home catalogs. Someday they will go through
their wardrobes and mark certain items for tentative mending
and certain items for passing on to relatives of similar shape
and size. Someday sloppy people will make family scrapbooks
into which they will put newspaper clippings, postcards, locks
of hair, and the dried corsage from their senior prom. Someday
they will file everything on the surface of their desk, including
the cash receipts from coffee purchases at the snack shop.
Someday they will sit down and read all the back issues of *The
New Yorker.*

4   For all these noble reasons and more, sloppy people never
get neat. They aim too high and wide. They save everything,
planning someday to file, order, and straighten out the world.
But while these ambitious plans take clearer and clearer shape
in their heads, the books spill from the shelves onto the floor,
the clothes pile up in the hamper and closet, the family me-
mentos accumulate in every drawer, the surface of the desk is
buried under mounds of paper and the unread magazines
threaten to reach the ceiling.

5   Sloppy people can't bear to part with anything. They give
loving attention to every detail. When sloppy people say
they're going to tackle the surface of the desk, they really mean
it. Not a paper will go unturned, not a rubber band will go un-
boxed. Four hours or two weeks into their excavation, the desk
looks exactly the same, primarily because the sloppy person is
meticulously creating new piles of papers with new headings
and scrupulously stopping to read all the old book catalogs before he throws them away. A neat person would just bulldoze
the desk.

6   Neat people are bums and clods at heart. They have cavalier
attitudes toward possessions, including family heirlooms.
Everything is just another dust-catcher to them. If anything col-
lects dust, it's got to go and that's that. Neat people will toy
with the idea of throwing the children out of the house just to
cut down on the clutter.

7   Neat people don't care about process. They like results. What they want to do is get the whole thing over with so they can sit down and watch the rasslin' on TV. Neat people operate on two unvarying principles: Never handle any item twice, and throw everything away.

8   The only thing messy in a neat person's house is the trash can. The minute something comes to a neat person's hand, he will look at it, try to decide if it has immediate use and, finding none, throw it in the trash.

9   Neat people are especially vicious with mail. They never go through their mail unless they are standing directly over a trash can. If the trash can is beside the mailbox, even better. All ads, catalogs, pleas for charitable contributions, church bulletins and money-saving coupons go straight into the trash can without being opened. All letters from home, postcards from Europe, bills and paychecks are opened, immediately responded to, then dropped in the trash can. Neat people keep their receipts only for tax purposes. That's it. No sentimental salvaging of birthday cards or the last letter a dying relative ever wrote. Into the trash it goes.

10   Neat people place neatness above everything, even economics. They are incredibly wasteful. Neat people throw away several toys every time they walk through the den. I knew a neat person once who threw away a perfectly good dish drainer because it had mold on it. The drainer was too much trouble to wash. And neat people sell their furniture when they move. They will sell a La-Z-Boy recliner while you are reclining in it.

11   Neat people are no good to borrow from. Neat people buy everything in expensive little single portions. They get their flour and sugar in two-pound bags. They wouldn't consider clipping a coupon, saving a leftover, reusing plastic nondairy whipped cream containers or rinsing off tin foil and draping it over the unmoldy dish drainer. You can never borrow a neat person's newspaper to see what's playing at the movies. Neat people have the paper all wadded up and in the trash by 7:05 A.M.

12   Neat people cut a clean swath through the organic as well as the inorganic world. People, animals, and things are all one to them. They are so insensitive. After they've finished with the pantry, the medicine cabinet and the attic, they will throw out the red geranium (too many leaves), sell the dog (too many fleas), and send the children off to boarding school (too many scuff marks on the hardwood floors).

Exercise 1 Discussion and Critical Thinking

(Review Comparison and Contrast, page 24.)

1. Is this essay mainly comparison or contrast?

2. Is Britt trying mainly to inform or to persuade?

3. What are the main points of this essay?

4. Is the pattern mainly point by point or subject by subject?

5. What is the moral distinction between neat people and sloppy people?

6. Britt says that sloppy people are morally superior to neat people. How does that idea differ from common assumptions?

7. To what extent is Britt serious, and to what extent is she just being humorous?

8. Britt presents two extremes. What qualities would a person in the middle have?

The Messy Are in Denial

Joyce Gallagher

> *Freelance journalist Joyce Gallagher gives us some insights into why the disorganized often marry the organized. She says it's all part of a design in Nature. Reasoning and her personal experience tell her so.*

1   Others may see the disorganized as carefree people wallowing happily in the cluttered chaos of their own making. I see

their conduct for what it so obviously is—a crying out for help. If they are so contented, then why are so many of them latching onto and becoming entirely dependent on those of us who are organized? Complaining all the while about being controlled they, nevertheless, behave like mistletoe nailing itself to oaks, fleas colonizing St. Bernards, and funguses invading feet.

2   That tendency is easy to document and understand. Anyone can see why the disorganized (the messy, the sloppy, the disorderly, the Pisces, the idealist, the daydreamer) need the organized (the orderly, the systematic, the tidy, the Virgo, the neat, the realistic, the practical). But that leaves the more complicated question: Why would the organized even tolerate the disorganized? Or to use our figures of speech, why would oaks, St. Bernards, and feet be so submissive? I say the answer to all such connections can be found in the phrase "balance in nature." Every creature-type occupies a niche or plunges into extinction. One role of those who are neat (while they are enjoying their own practical and artistic triumphs) is to provide a secure directive system so the sloppy can experience their measure of fulfillment. Like a stoical whale with a barnacle, the organized hang in there while the disorganized hang on.

3   Of course, hanging on, or even hanging around, doesn't mean the disorganized are always complete parasites. Far from it. In fact, the disorganized are often writers, artists, musicians, pop philosophers, and lovable flakes. They may even be fun to be around, even get married to—even stay married to, if you can get past their messiness.

4   If you will just listen, the disorganized will explain *ad nauseam* their lives as works in progress. And in a sense their lives are works in progress, not in advanced stages of progress such as revision or editing, but in freewriting, brainstorming, clustering. Without a thesis, they freewrite through the material world, not yet knowing what to keep or discard. They brainstorm through life, jumping from one acquisition to another, clustering their "treasures" in attics, work rooms, garages, and other handy, unprotected spaces. Finally, if not directed by an organized person, they run the risk of inundating themselves with their own junk.

5   Fortunately, when Nature has its way, an organizer comes to the rescue—as a friend, a relative, or, perhaps, an official. In my situation. I'm the organized spouse, sometimes succumbing to my disorganized companion's pathetic romanticism, but more often, saving him from himself.

6   I do what I can. As he busily accumulates, I busily distrib-
ute. It's not easy. Toil as I might, I look around and see him
effortlessly acquiring, like a tornado sucking in stuff faster
than I can throw it away. I especially donate to thrift stores.
Hapless children, the disabled of all kinds, and veterans of all
wars depend mightily on us organized people to provide mer-
chandise to their benefactors. Unfortunately for the organized,
the thrift industry also depends on the disorganized as customers to cart home items such as scratchy records, manual
typewriters, vintage clothing, and myriad unspeakable arti-
facts called "collectibles."

7   And if it's not a thrift store providing a game preserve for
the disorganized, it's a yard sale. Organized people conduct yard
sales. The disorganized attend them. As slack-jawed, hollow-
eyed hulks, they drive compulsively from one location to another, not knowing what they are looking for. I suppose it's an
ancient yearning for the hunt, even when the belly, larder, and
garage are full. I've known my significant disorganized other to
stake out a promising sale site a full hour before opening time,
peering through the windshield of his motorized blind, stalking
the forlorn, unwanted inanimate prey. Way back in the distance, I shovel out junk, knowing it is the burden of the neat to
offset every shopping binge of the sloppy.

8   Despite my taking credit for rescuing and sustaining my
disorganized mate, pride didn't prompt me to write this. In fact,
I don't particularly relish my lot as an organized person with a
directive mission. My behavior is quite beyond my control. As
mentioned previously, it's probably instinctive, genetic. Tens of
thousands of evolutionary years have made my opposite and me
what we are.

9   My spouse's counterpart was perhaps an ancient daydream-
ing troglodyte, who decorated sandstone cave walls with draw-
ings of hunts, imagining the glories of bringing down that mam-
moth with one club whomp. If so, there was a well-groomed
organizer in the background, arranging his clubs all in a row and
his life generally. If she hadn't done so, he couldn't have contributed to the diverse gene pool into which we now dip.

10   Reason tells me that's what happened to the Neanderthals—
there was too much inbreeding among the disorganized. Consider the artists' uniform depictions of these creatures: messy to
the max, with grubby fingers and tousled hair, their privates
barely concealed by scrappy animal-hide clothing. It's no wonder

science has failed to establish kinship between them and the surviving relatively neat- and tidy-looking *homo sapiens.*

Exercise 2   Discussion and Critical Thinking

(Review Comparison and Contrast, page 24.)

1. Is this essay mostly comparison or contrast?

2. Is Gallagher trying mostly to inform or to persuade?

3. What points of contrast are applied to the two types?

4. How much truth do you find amid the humor?

5. Do you agree that disorganized people need organized people?

6. Can one also make the point that organized people need disorganized people?

7. Can the high rate of divorce be partly traced to how organized people and disorganized people do or do not pair up?

Exercise 3   Connecting the Readings

1. In comparing the two essays, what subjects are equivalent?

2. Britt says that neat people are lazy and mean. Does Gallagher say anything similar about disorganized people? If Gallagher doesn't go that far, then how far does she go in characterizing the disorganized?

3. Are the differences mainly in the types (neat and messy) being discussed or in the interpretation of the two types?

4. Both authors use humor to exaggerate traits. Which author distorts reality more?

5. Which author seems more flexible? Explain.

6. With which side of which comparison do you identify, if at all? Why?

✳ Reading-Related Writing

"Neat People vs. Sloppy People"

(See Comparison and Contrast, page 24.)

1. Using ideas and points from this essay, discuss two people you know or have read about to argue that Britt's conclusions are valid.
2. Using ideas and points from this essay, discuss two people you know or have read about to argue that her ideas are not valid.
3. Write a comparative study on people with good table manners and those with poor table manners. Explain the causes and effects of their behavior.
4. Using Britt's essay as a model of exaggerated humor, write a comparative study of one of the following:

   - People who exercise a lot and those who hardly exercise
   - People who diet and those who do not
   - Men with beards and those without
   - Women with extremely long fingernails and those with short fingernails
   - People who dye their hair and those who do not
   - People who take care of their yards and those who do not
   - People who take care of their children (or pets) and those who do not

"The Messy Are in Denial"

5. Using Gallagher's points and insights, discuss two people you know or have read about to argue that her conclusions are valid.
6. Using Gallagher's points and insights, discuss two people you know or have read about to argue that her ideas are not valid.

Combined Reading Selections

7. Compare and contrast Britt's sloppy person with Gallagher's disorganized person.
8. Compare and contrast Britt's neat person with Gallagher's organized person.

Writing on the Wall

Ask graffitists if they would mind if we spray-paint symbols on their cars, walls, and homes. Then ask anti-graffitists how they would feel if Picasso were to return to life and proceed to decorate their cars, walls, and homes with spray paint. Then, answers in hand, write an essay about graffiti. Or just read the following articles about "writing on walls," and let your words fly.

Hint: For college essay assignments, most instructors prefer that you use a computer printer rather than a spray can.

- "Graffiti: Taking a Closer Look" advances the "broken windows" theory: that graffiti is a threshold act leading to deteriorating property values and living conditions.
- "Creepin' While You're Sleepin'" puts you on the dark streets in the dead of night and provides a scary and realistic ride-along study of a dedicated graffitist, who just happens to be a female.

Graffiti: Taking a Closer Look

Christopher Grant

First published as a cover story in the FBI Law Enforcement Bulletin, *this article is included as general-interest material in InfoTrac, a data service provider mainly for libraries. It offers a thorough analysis, but it also takes an argumentative position. See how it corresponds with your own views.*

1   Not long ago, the word *graffiti* conjured images of innocent messages, such as "Tom loves Jane" or "Class of '73." Such simple and innocuous scribblings, although occasionally still seen, have become essentially messages of the past. Most of the graffiti that mars contemporary American landscape—both urban and rural—contains messages of hatred, racism, and gang warfare. Public attitudes toward graffiti tend to fluctuate between indifference and intolerance. On a national level, the criminal justice system has yet to adopt a uniform response to graffiti and the individuals who create this so-called street art. While some juris-

dictions combat the problem aggressively, others do very little or nothing at all to punish offenders or to deter the spread of graffiti.

2   To a large degree, society's inability to decide on a focused response to graffiti stems from the nature of the offense. It could be argued that graffiti falls into the grey area between crime and public nuisance. If graffiti is considered in a vacuum, such an argument could appear to have some credence. However, it is unrealistic, and ultimately foolhardy, to view such a public offense in a vacuum. There is a growing consensus in communities around the country that the problem of graffiti, if left unaddressed, creates an environment where other more serious crimes flourish and can quickly degrade once low-crime areas. At a time when law enforcement agencies nationwide are adopting more community-based policing philosophies, administrators are exploring ways to address the basic factors that lead to crime and neighborhood decline. The time has come to take a closer look at graffiti.

Wall Writing

3   *Graffiti* is general term for wall writing, perhaps humankind's earliest art form. The crude wall writings of prehistoric times and the highly stylized street art of today's inner-city youths share one common feature: Each stems from a basic human need to communicate with others. For youths who may not be able to express themselves through other media, such as prose or music, graffiti represents an easily accessible and effective way to communicate with a large audience. Anyone can obtain a can of spray paint and "make their mark" on a highway overpass or the side of a building.

4   Modern graffiti generally falls into one of three categories— junk graffiti, gang graffiti, and tagging. *Junk graffiti* messages are not gang-related but often involve obscene, racist, or threatening themes. The line separating gang graffiti and tagging has become blurred in recent years. *Tagging,* once seen as a nonviolent alternative to more threatening gang activities, is now considered an entry level offense that can lead to more serious crimes, including burglary and assault. In addition, tagging often results in direct gang affiliation. While all types of graffiti threaten the quality of life in affected areas, tagging and graffiti tied to gang activities represent the most widespread and formidable challenges to communities around the country.

Tagging

5   Tagging as a form of graffiti first appeared in the early 1980s and has grown immensely popular in many parts of the country, in both rural and urban areas. A tagger is someone who adopts a nickname, or tag, and then writes it on as many surfaces as possible, usually in highly visible locations. Although spray paint is the most common medium, taggers—sometimes referred to as "piecers," "writers," and "hip-hop artists"—also may use magic markers or etching tools to create their images.

6   The motivation behind tagging involves fame, artistic expression, power, and rebellion—all integral parts of what has been referred to as the hip-hop culture. Tagging may fill an even deeper void for youths without a strong sense of personal identity. Interviews with taggers reveal a deep desire simply to be known, to create an identity for themselves, and to communicate it to others. The thrill of risktaking also appears to be an underlying motivation for many taggers. While the images taggers create may not necessarily be gang-related, research shows that most taggers hope to join gangs and use tagging as a way to gain the attention of gang members. The more often their monikers appear in different locations, the more publicity they receive. Consequently, a small number of taggers can cause a disproportionate amount of property damage in a community. Tagging messages usually resemble handwriting, but may be difficult, if not impossible, to read. Taggers also have been known to invent their own letters or symbols, often adding to the confusion over the message and the author. . . .

Communication and Territoriality

7   In an article about the increase in area gang violence, a local California newspaper accurately described graffiti as a "crude but effective way for gang members to communicate among themselves, with the community, and with rival gangs." Communication is an important attribute of graffiti that law enforcement and community leaders should understand as they attempt to address the problem. While neighborhood residents and police might see graffiti simply as a blight, gang members and many taggers view it not so much as property damage but as a means to send messages understood within the gang community.

8   The expressive value of graffiti also forms an important component of gang territoriality. Gangs, and potential gang members, use graffiti to identify and mark their territory. Although the traditional perception of gang territoriality has been altered by increased mobility via the automobile, research of a noted gang expert indicates that gangs continue to "mark, define, claim, protect, and fight over their turf." In fact, territoriality among rival gangs continues to be a major source of gang violence. Graffiti as a primary form of communication and turf identification plays a direct part in feeding this violence.

True Impact of Graffiti

9   The threat posed by graffiti to neighborhoods and society in general goes much deeper than territorial gang violence. Community leaders need only to consider the reverberating effects of graffiti to understand how a seemingly low-grade misdemeanor can threaten or destroy the quality of life in an entire community. The monetary damages attributed to graffiti speak for themselves. In one year, the City of Los Angeles spent more than $15 million on graffiti eradication. This figure does not include the volunteer time devoted to graffiti cleanup or the estimated millions of dollars spent by private businesses taking care of the problem themselves. In addition, the Southern California Rapid Transit District spent $12 million on graffiti removal during the same year. . . .

10   James Q. Wilson, UCLA criminologist and framer of the "broken windows" theory, states that signs of disorder in society—such as graffiti, abandoned cars, broken windows, and uncollected trash—frighten law-abiding citizens into avoiding public places. Those places are then left to criminals who further deface them, creating a downward spiral in which the fear of crime leads to an increase in criminal activity. The presence of graffiti discourages citizens from shopping or living in affected areas. As established businesses relocate or close, new businesses might be reluctant to move into areas where customers would feel unsafe. As property values decline and law-abiding citizens with resources move, once-thriving neighborhoods can quickly degrade into dangerous places. Thus, the seemingly trivial offense of graffiti ultimately can have devastating consequences for a community.

Response

11   Most experts agree that allowing graffiti to remain visible in a community sends a message that this type of behavior is acceptable to residents. Further, allowing graffiti in an area encourages other offenders to degrade the community with more graffiti or other acts of vandalism. As stated in a newspaper article, ". . . removing graffiti as soon as it appears is the best way to deter further vandalism."

12   Recognizing the serious threat posed by graffiti, a number of communities across the country have developed programs to respond to the problem. The City of Anaheim, California, is considered a leader in developing innovative programs dealing with taggers and the damage they cause. The city developed "Adopt-a-Block" and "Wipeout Graffiti" programs and also established a 24-hour graffiti hotline that encourages residents to report graffiti damage, as well as information about suspects. Information leading to an arrest and conviction can net the caller up to $500. The hotline has proven to be quite successful. To date, callers have received more than $16,500 for information provided about offenders. The courts sentence convicted taggers to perform community service that includes graffiti removal. Anaheim also adopted an antigraffiti ordinance that assigns responsibility for the cost of graffiti removal to taggers, prohibits possession of implements used to create graffiti, and requires merchants to keep aerosol spray cans or other implements used to create graffiti out of direct reach of the general public. . . . To enhance graffiti-related investigations, Orange County, California, uses a forensic scientist specializing in handwriting analysis to help identify chronic offenders. Several other localities in California have passed ordinances calling for convicted taggers to perform up to 80 hours of graffiti removal as part of their sentences.

The Future

13   Although these approaches represent a step in the right direction, they are reactive measures and do little to address the causes of the graffiti problem. The causes lie deep within the roots of social structure; it will require much more than rollers and paint to correct the problem.

14   One of the first steps is to educate the public about graffiti—its meaning and its potential impact on a community. Citizens

must understand that this type of behavior cannot be tolerated because its insidious nature threatens communities from within. To deter new graffiti, young people should be taught that their actions can have far-reaching consequences. Law enforcement agencies may consider augmenting drug- and gang-prevention efforts with lessons on graffiti. Students should be advised that damaging property with graffiti is a serious crime and offenders will be punished. As part of the lesson, instructors also may suggest and encourage alternative methods of self-expression.

Conclusion

15   Like prostitution and illegal gambling, people often view graffiti as a victimless crime. But as communities around the country have learned, there is no such thing as a victimless crime. In fact, crimes that do not produce a single, identifiable victim generally have more impact on the entire community. As a highly visible offense, graffiti represents a particularly menacing threat to the quality of life in a community. The residual effects of reduced property values, lost business, increased gang territoriality, and heightened fear of crime escalate the severity of graffiti related offenses beyond their impact as visual pollution. Communities that do not develop measures to deter and prevent graffiti now may find themselves confronting more intractable problems in the future.

Exercise 1 Discussion and Critical Thinking

1. Underline the sentence in paragraph 2 that indicates what the author is trying to do.

2. Underline the sentence in paragraph 4 that takes a clear position on graffiti and, therefore, can be called the proposition.

3. Draw vertical lines in the left margin to indicate the sentences in paragraphs 1 and 2 that tie this essay to an audience concerned with law enforcement.

4. According to Grant, what motivates taggers?

5. Why do many gang members do graffiti?

6. What is the "broken windows" theory?

7. What form of writing is used in paragraph 10?

8. What is the best way to deter further graffiti?

9. What should be done to deal with the causes of graffiti problems?

10. Does the solution of educating young people about the problems caused by graffiti suggest that the writer has faith in human beings? Why or why not?

11. What parts do you agree and not agree with? Explain.

12. If you could add one more strong section (or strengthen one), what would it be?

Creepin' While You're Sleepin'

Stephen Lemons

> *Unwilling to write about graffiti just from looking at it or researching it, freelance author Stephen Lemons rode along with a graffiti posse, listening to their views, to the hiss of spray cans under the canopy of darkness. The leader is a girl graffiti bomber and heartbreaker named Tribe, who paints the town and fears no cops.*

1   It's close to 2 A.M. on a cold spring morning, and Tribe and her fellow graffiti artists Zes and Revok have gone into the

24-hour Home Depot on Sunset Boulevard in Hollywood to rack some cans for a bombing run. When they march out into the almost empty parking lot, Tribe's clutching a spray-paint can and wearing a smile that all but reads, "Mission accomplished." She hops in a sweet white Mustang with her homeboys and they take off for the 'hood.

2   "Even if I have money on me, I'll still rack," the petite, copper-skinned 21-year-old explains a few moments prior to this bit of petty larceny. "I love the rush. I like adrenaline and vandalism. Anything I'm not supposed to do, I like doing."

3   Racking, for those unfamiliar with the parlance, means stealing. In this instance, racking specifically refers to shoplifting spray paint for a night of intense tagging, known as bombing in the graffiti subculture. Racking is pretty common in the graffiti world, and some stores, knowing this, lock up their cans. But it seems sort of silly to go to such effort to protect a product that usually runs about $2. Hell, they might as well give it away.

4   "I'm not scared of cops," says Tribe, who lives with her mom and sister in an area of La-La Land she wishes to keep under wraps. "But I know they have the right to put me in jail. I'm not afraid of jail, either, but I don't want to spend a lot of time there."

5   By her own account, this attractive, half-Japanese/half-Native American girl has done a few short stints behind bars. She's been picked up several times for tagging and did a week in Sybil Brand Institute under a fake name. According to Tribe, she's on probation for whatever she did last. If the cops catch her again, it means three years in the pokey. Because she wisely refuses to give out her full name, none of this can be checked.

6   Whatever her rap sheet looks like, her rep in the mostly male graffiti community is solid. Graff writers in San Francisco, San Diego, New York, and L.A. all know Tribe. San Francisco writer Twist, a.k.a. Barry McGee, whose work has graced the cover of the art mag *Juxtapoz* as well as the walls of the influential New York gallery Deitch Projects and the UCLA Hammer Museum (not to mention quite a few freight trains), calls Tribe "legendary." That's high praise in the writing community. Perhaps the highest.

7   Aside from the props, Tribe's also on the current cover of *Big Time,* the slick, underground graffiti rag out of Glendale. The shot shows Tribe, in shorts and a tube top, writing her

name in white spray paint on the front driver's side window of a Metro bus. She hopped up on the front fender while it paused at a stop so the photographer could snap it. Of course, her face is not visible. Still, you have to admit, it takes some *cojones* to pull a stunt like that.

8   *Big Time's* contents page pays homage with this caption: "One of L.A.'s hardest hitters earns her respect not based on the fact that she's female (no special treatment here, kiddies), but because she has been up consistently since the early '90s. In fact, she's been known to hit spots so sickening that many of the baddest dudes in the industry have to take a step back and shake their heads helplessly. Oh yeah—for all you haters out there, the flick is real and taken inservice. Dig?!"

9   One photo does not a legend make. Tribe became part of graffiti's elite through the sweat of her pretty brow and the kind of monomaniacal obsession with the game that only another writer would understand. More of a bomber-tagger than a piecer (a species of writer known for painting large, multicolored "masterpieces"), Tribe gets up and stays up by going out almost every night from 2 A.M., when the nightclub where she waits tables cuts her loose, until six or seven in the morning. She nabs the supertight spots on rooftops, overpasses, and billboards, risking her neck in the process. She's been hard at it for eight years, since she was 13 years old.

10   "For one person to go out and do all the shit that she's done is a lot, let alone for being a little girl," says friend and fellow writer Toomer. "Especially in the tough areas she's bombed: South Central, Watts, Compton, Inglewood. She could get raped by gangs and shit if she got caught. But she always seems to talk her way out of it."

11   Toomer is the leader of TKO, a notorious outfit that he describes as half "hard-core" members living the gang lifestyle in Pacoima and half writers in L.A. He's also a member, along with Tribe and other big names like Saber and Revok, of MSK, which stands for "Mad Society Kings." MSK is a tight crew comprising the hardest bombers in the city. Toomer claims TKO and MSK are reviled by the police, and he ain't talkin' smack. Even a cursory glance around the city reveals an abundance of their markings.

12   "A lot of guys won't admit that a woman kicks much ass," says Toomer. "But she gets some spots that make motherfuckers'

balls go in. I've been doing this graffiti shit for 13 years straight. My life means nothing but graffiti, and I know who's coming and going. No other female on the West Coast bombs like that.

13   "That bitch is crazy," he adds. "I mean, I'm aware that graffiti is illegal, but sometimes I wonder if she does. She's either an airhead or she just doesn't give a fuck."

Tribe doesn't strike you as an airhead, but she does know how to play men. She comes off as a sweet, innocent kid, though down deep she's as tough as an alley cat. If you ask, she'll tell you all about getting an A.A. degree from the Fashion Institute of Design and Merchandising and wanting to snag a job in fashion or the arts. Listening to all this it's hard not to feel avuncular toward her. She elicits that protectiveness from men without effort. As you might expect, this comes in handy when dealing with Officer Friendly.

14   "I've been caught a lot of times," she confesses. "But that's the one benefit of being a girl. They usually let me go."

15   The first time she realized the advantages nature bestowed upon her, she was bombing with Revok and got "sweated" (stopped but not arrested) by the cops. As a black-and-white shined a light on her, she shouted for Revok to run. She had paint all over her hands, but the bulls just gave her a lecture about how she shouldn't be hanging out with the "wrong" type of guys. Then they took off to look in vain for Revok. Tribe suddenly realized what "girl power" was all about. However, there's a downside to being a female player in the male chauvinist world of tagging.

16   "Other writers will say, 'She's good for a girl,'" explains Tribe. "Or they'll talk shit about you. Most guys think girls are only for one thing. So it's hard to get respect. That's kinda why I chose the name Tribe. I wanted to be respected as a writer, not as a girl."

17   Respect she has. But Tribe's also got the attention of many a male writer who'd like to get next to her. Indeed, for the artistic, street-tough youths who take to graffiti, she's a not-so-obscure object of hormone-driven desires.

18   "She's fuckin' pretty, dude," says San Diego writer Chie Rock. "It's cool to see girls out there bombing, who aren't afraid. Graffiti is like screaming. But you're screaming to the streets. I think she's hurtin' inside. She needs someone to hold her, dude. That's what I think."

19   Maybe, Chie, but good luck trying. Tribe the adrenaline junkie doesn't sit still for very long, and she has enough ambition to fill the L.A. River bed. Plus, she won't be stopping anytime soon. Unless, of course, she gets nailed by The Man.

20   Stephen Powers, the outlaw author of *The Art of Getting Over* (St. Martin's Press), a book considered to be the graffiti bible and one that gets racked by its fans as often as it gets bought, writes that graffiti is "heroic in our couch-potato culture." If that's the case, Tribe's efforts are doubly heroic because of her gender.

21   Asked if girl writers are rare, Powers is emphatic. "Hell yeah," he replies in an e-mail. "Reas (another great graffiti writer) made the observation once, 'Girls hate the violence.' And, unfortunately, that's an ever-present threat." So is the law. As Tribe's Mustang cruises further south, it passes the Rampart cop shop—home of the cowboys who are costing L.A. all those millions for busting heads and framing suspects. But it doesn't seem to bother Tribe and her homies. They stop before a mostly blank stretch of wall, jump out of the car, and start to rock that spot with a furious, almost insane intensity. A clean commercial truck nearby gets the same treatment. It sways from side to side as the taggers crawl all over that baby, leaving it tattooed with the maniacal hieroglyphics of modern urban youth.

22   One feels for the truck's driver when he gets up in the morning. One's also awestruck at the fearlessness Tribe and her posse display. Both the truck and the wall are in plain view of passing traffic. Despite the late hour, that police station is just around the corner. You'd have to have ice in your veins for the hair on the back of your neck not to stand up. But Tribe seems oblivious to any threat.

23   "I really enjoy bombing," she says in a sweet, matter-of-fact tone. "When I'm out there bombing, I kind of forget about everything else in the world. All I care about is getting the spot. When I step back and see it, I feel proud of myself."

24   Later that evening, Tribe says, she got sweated by a CHP officer while she was tagging a tunnel. Revok and Zes were nearby, but not in the patrolman's line of vision. So there was Tribe alone for the moment with can in hand. Seeing a young woman in a dark tunnel by herself late at night, the cop asked if she was all right. When Tribe said yes, he took off.

25   "Cool, huh?" she asks. Cool? Hey, you be the judge.

Exercise 2 Discussion and Critical Thinking

1. Why does Tribe "rack"?

2. How well-known is Tribe?

3. Which is more likely to be called artistic, at least by intention—
   a piecer or a bomber-tagger?

4. In addition to tagging, what else does Tribe want to do with her
   life?

5. In what way is this article about a struggle for equality?

6. How do you feel about Stephen Powers's view that graffiti is
   "heroic in our couch-potato culture"?

7. Does Lemons seem to be moved more by the plight of the driver
   whose vehicle is tagged, or by the "fearlessness" of the posse?

8. How do you think the posse would have reacted if someone had
   tagged that "sweet white Mustang" while they were tagging the
   truck?

✳ Reading-Related Writing

"Graffiti: Taking a Closer Look"

(See Argument, page 28, and Cause and Effect, page 21.)

1. Write an argument about the intentions and benefits of art in
   graffiti.
2. Write an argument in which you take issue with any part of the
   essay by Grant.

3. Write an essay generally in agreement with Grant, using your own examples to refer to neighborhoods or towns that have been damaged by graffiti. (See Exemplification, page 18.)
4. If you know people who do or have done graffiti, interview them with questions framed around Grant's argument. Then write an essay of argument that incorporates or counters their views.

"Creepin' While You're Sleepin'"

5. Write an essay in which you discuss Tribe's character traits you like and those you dislike. (See Analysis by Division, page 18.)
6. If you mostly dislike Tribe's behavior, discuss her character traits that she could redirect to something more constructive. (See Cause and Effect, page 21.)
7. In an essay use references to and quotations from this article, and perhaps from the previous article by Grant, to support your views on graffiti. (See Argument, page 28, and Exemplification, page 18.)
8. Write an essay in which you speculate about what would be Tribe's reaction to the main points in "Graffiti: Taking a Closer Look." (See Comparison and Contrast, page 24.)

8

Workplaces from Hell

If you're in a workplace from hell, you may wonder how it acquired that infamy. It's probably not the heat, it's the humans—specifically your peers and bosses.

These two essays will provide you with some insights and solutions for predicaments you've been in, are in, or—probably, some sad day—will be in:

- "How to Deal with a Difficult Boss" describes the methods of operation of inept managers and arms you with survival techniques.
- "Coworkers from Hell and How to Cope" is a primer for understanding and neutralizing the annoying peers you can't avoid or annihilate.

How to Deal with a Difficult Boss

Donna Brown Hogarty

> *Journalist Donna Brown Hogarty makes it clear that if you've ever had a boss, you've had a bad boss in certain respects. Bosses who are particularly bad, she says, can be grouped in five categories; and being able to recognize the kind of bad boss you have is the first step in dealing with discomfort and frustration at work.*

1   Harvey Gittler knew his new boss was high-strung—the two had worked together on the factory floor. But Gittler was not prepared for his co-worker's personality change when the man was promoted to plant manager.

2   Just two days later, the boss angrily ordered a standing desk removed because he'd seen a worker leaning on it to look up an order. He routinely dressed down employees at the top of his lungs. At one time or another he threatened to fire almost everyone in the plant. And after employees went home, he searched through trash cans for evidence of treason.

3   For many workers, Gittler's experience is frighteningly familiar. Millions of Americans have temperamental bosses. In a

1984 Center for Creative Leadership study of corporate executives, nearly 75 percent of the subjects reported having had at least one intolerable boss.

4   "Virtually all bosses are problem bosses, in one way or another," says psychologist Mardy Grothe, co-author with Peter Wylie of *Problem Bosses: Who They Are and How to Deal with Them.* The reason, he said, lies in lack of training. Most bosses were promoted to management because they excelled at earlier jobs—not because they have experience motivating others.

5   Uncertain economic times worsen the bad-boss syndrome. "There is an acceptance of getting results at any price," says Stanley Bing, a business executive and author of *Crazy Bosses.* "As a result, the people corporations select to be bosses are the most rigid and demanding, and the least able to roll with the punches."

6   Bad bosses often have a recognizable *modus operandi.* Harry Levinson, a management psychologist in Waltham, Massachusetts, has catalogued problem bosses, from the bully to the jellyfish to the disapproving perfectionist. If you're suffering from a bad boss, chances are he or she combines several of these traits and can be dealt with effectively if you use the right strategy.

The Bully

7   During his first week on the job, a new account manager at a small Pennsylvania advertising agency agreed to return some materials to a client. When he mentioned this at a staff meeting, the boss turned beet red, his lips began to quiver and he shouted that the new employee should call his client and confess he didn't know anything about the advertising business, and would *not* be returning the materials.

8   Over the next few months, as the account manager watched co-workers cower under the boss's browbeating, he realized that the tyrant fed on fear. Employees who tried hardest to avoid his ire were most likely to catch it. "He was like a schoolyard bully," the manager recalls, "and I've known since childhood that, when confronted, most bullies back down."

9   Armed with new-found confidence and growing knowledge of the ad business, he matched his boss's behavior. "If he raised his voice, I'd raise mine," the manager recalls. True to type, the boss started to treat him with grudging respect. Eventually, the young man moved up the ranks and was rarely subjected to his boss's outbursts.

10   Although standing up to the bully often works, it *could* make matters worse. Mardy Grothe recommends a different strategy: reasoning with him after he's calmed down. "Some bosses have had a problem with temper control all their lives, and are not pleased with this aspect of their personality," he explains. Want a litmus test? If the boss attempts to compensate for his outburst by overreacting and trying to "make nice" the next day, says Grothe, he or she feels guilty about yesterday's bad behavior.

11   Grothe suggests explaining to your boss how his temper affects you. For instance, you might say, "I know you're trying to improve my performance, but yelling makes me less productive because it upsets me."

12   Whatever strategy you choose, deal with the bully as soon as possible, because "once a dominant/subservient relationship is established, it becomes difficult to loosen," warns industrial psychologist James Fisher. Fisher also suggests confronting your boss behind closed doors whenever possible, to avoid being disrespectful. If your boss continues to be overbearing, try these strategies from psychologist Leonard Felder, author of *Does Someone at Work Treat You Badly?*

- To keep your composure while the boss is screaming, repeat a calming phrase to yourself, such as "Ignore the anger. It isn't yours."
- Focus on a humorous aspect of your boss's appearance. If she's got a double chin, watch her flesh shake while she's yammering. "By realizing that even the most intimidating people are vulnerable, you can more easily relax," explains Felder.
- Wait for your boss to take a breath, then try this comeback line: "I want to hear what you're saying. You've got to slow down."

13   Finally, never relax with an abusive boss, no matter how charming he or she can be, says Stanley Bing. "The bully will worm his or her way into your heart as a way of positioning your face under his foot."

The Workaholic

14   "Some bosses don't know the difference between work and play," says Nancy Ahlrichs, vice president of client services at the Indianapolis office of Right Associates, an international outplacement firm. "If you want to reach them at night or on a

Saturday, just call the office." Worse, such a boss invades your every waking hour, making it all but impossible to separate your own home life from the office.

15   Ahlrichs advises setting limits on your availability. Make sure the boss knows you can be reached in a crisis, but as a matter of practice go home at a set time. If he responds angrily, reassure him that you will tackle any project first thing in the morning. Get him to set the priorities, so you can decide which tasks can wait.

16   If you have good rapport with the boss, says Mardy Grothe, consider discussing the problem openly. Your goal is to convince him that just as he needs to meet deadlines, you have personal responsibilities that are equally important.

The Jellyfish

17   "My boss hires people with the assumption that we all know our jobs," says a woman who works for a small firm in New England. "Unfortunately, he hates conflict. If someone makes a mistake, we have to tiptoe around instead of moving to correct it, so we don't hurt anyone's feelings."

18   Her boss is a jellyfish. He has refused to establish even a basic pecking order in his office. As a result, a secretary sat on important correspondence for over a month, risking a client's tax write-offs. Because no one supervises the firm's support staff, the secretary never received a reprimand, and nobody was able to prevent such mishaps from recurring. The jellyfish simply can't take charge because he's afraid of creating conflicts.

19   So "*you* must take charge," suggests Lee Colby, a Minneapolis-based management consultant. "Tell the jellyfish: 'This is what I think I ought to be doing. What do you think?' You are taking the first step, without stepping on your boss's toes."

20   Building an indecisive supervisor's confidence is another good strategy. For example, if you can supply hard facts and figures, you can then use them to justify any course you recommend—and gently ease the jellyfish into taking a firmer position.

The Perfectionist

21   When Nancy Ahlrichs was fresh out of college, she landed her first full-time job, supervising the advertising design and layout of a small-town newspaper. On deadline day, the paper's irritable general manager would suddenly appear over her

shoulder, inspecting her work for errors. Then he'd ask a barrage of questions, ending with the one Ahlrichs dreaded most: "Are you sure you'll make deadline?"

22   "I never missed a single deadline," Ahlrichs says, "yet every week he'd ask that same question. I felt belittled by his lack of confidence in me."

23   Ironically, the general manager was lowering the staff's productivity. To paraphrase Voltaire, the perfect is the enemy of the good. According to psychiatrist Allan Mallinger, co-author with Jeannette DeWyze of *Too Perfect: When Being in Control Gets Out of Control,* "The perfectionist's overconcern for thoroughness slows down everyone's work. When everything has to be done perfectly, tasks loom larger." The nit-picking boss who is behind schedule becomes even more difficult, making subordinates ever more miserable.

24   "Remember," says Leonard Felder, "the perfectionist *needs* to find something to worry about." To improve your lot with a perfectionist boss, get her to focus on the big picture. If she demands that you redo a task you've just completed, mention your other assignments, and ask her to prioritize. Often, a boss will let the work you've completed stand—especially when she realizes another project may be put on hold. If your boss is nervous about a particular project, offer regular reports. By keeping the perfectionist posted, you might circumvent constant supervision.

25   Finally, protect yourself emotionally. "You can't depend on the perfectionist for encouragement," says Mallinger. "You owe it to yourself to get a second opinion of your work by asking others."

The Aloof Boss

26   When Gene Bergoffen, now CEO of the National Private Truck Council, worked for another trade association and asked to be included in the decision-making process, his boss was brusque and inattentive. The boss made decisions alone, and very quickly. "We used to call him 'Ready, Fire, Aim,'" says Bergoffen.

27   Many workers feel frozen out by their boss in subtle ways. Perhaps he doesn't invite them to key meetings or he might never be available to discuss projects. "At the core of every good boss is the ability to communicate expectations clearly," says Gerard Roche, chairman of Heidrick & Struggles, an executive

search firm. "Employees should never have to wonder what's on a boss's mind."

28   If your boss fails to give you direction, Roche says, "the worst thing you can do is nothing. Determine the best course of action, then say to your boss: 'Unless I hear otherwise, here's what I'm going to do.'"

29   Other strategies: When your boss does not invite you to meetings or include you in decision making, speak up. "Tell her you have information that might prove to be valuable," suggests Lee Colby. If that approach doesn't work, find an intermediary who respects your work and can persuade the boss to listen to your views.

30   To understand your boss's inability to communicate, it's vital to examine his work style. "Some like hard data, logically arranged in writing," says Colby. "Others prefer face-to-face meetings. Find out what makes your boss tick—and speak in his or her language."

31   Understanding your boss can make your job more bearable in a number of ways. For instance, try offering the boss two solutions to a problem—one that will make him happy, and one that will help you to reach your goals. Even the most difficult boss will usually allow you to solve problems in your own way—as long as he's convinced of your loyalty to him.

32   No matter which type of bad boss you have, think twice before going over his head. Try forming a committee with your colleagues and approaching the boss all together. The difficult boss is usually unaware of the problem and often is eager to make amends.

33   Before embarking on any course of action, engage in some self-analysis. Chances are, no matter how difficult your job is, you are also contributing to the conflict. "Talk to people who know you both, and get some honest feedback," suggests Mardy Grothe. "If you can fix the ways in which you're contributing to the problem, you'll be more likely to get your boss to change."

34   Even if you can't, there's a silver lining: the worst bosses often have the most to teach you. Bullies, for example, are frequently masters at reaching difficult goals. Perfectionists can often prod you into exceeding your own expectations.

35   As a young resident psychologist at the Menninger psychiatric hospital in Topeka, Kansas, Harry Levinson was initially overwhelmed by the high standards of founder Karl Menninger.

"I felt I was never going to be able to diagnose patients as well as he did or perform to such high academic requirements," Levinson recalls. He even considered quitting. But in the end, he rose to the challenge, and today he believes he owes much of his success to what he learned during that critical period.

36   Dealing with a difficult boss forces you to set priorities, to overcome fears, to stay calm under the gun, and to negotiate for better working conditions. And the skills you sharpen to ease a tense relationship will stand you in good stead throughout your career. "Employees who are able to survive a trying boss often earn the respect of higher-ups for their ability to manage a situation," says Levinson. "And because a difficult boss can cause rapid turnover, those who stick it out often advance quickly."

37   Your bad boss can also teach you what *not* to do with subordinates as you move up—and one day enable you to be a better boss yourself.

Exercise 1   Discussion and Critical Thinking

1. What is being classified?

2. What is the purpose of the classification?

3. What are the five classes of bad bosses?

4. Of the five classes, which is the most difficult for most people to deal with? for you to deal with? Can you give any examples?

5. Hogarty suggests that sometimes the boss's behavior is caused to some extent by the behavior of the workers. How would you explain that? Provide examples, if possible.

6. Which of the five types of behavior are sometimes found in combination?

Coworkers from Hell and How to Cope

Erica Monfred

> *Not all types of coworkers are classified here by Erica Monfred.
> Just the ones from hell. Along with her classification, she pro-
> vides suggestions about how to send those obnoxious people
> back to their fiery place of origin. This essay was first published
> in* Cosmopolitan *in 1997.*

1   In every workplace, there are congenial, supportive colleagues. . . . and then there are the other kind—the ones you
fantasize about while pummeling the punching bag at the gym.
Is there an officemate sabotaging your success? Here is a primer
on how to handle the most common culprits.

1. Petty Bureaucrats

2   The petty bureaucrat is either the gatekeeper to someone
important or in charge of something everyone desperately
needs, like health insurance or paper clips. She doesn't actually
have the authority to get things done, but she does have the
power to prevent things from getting done.

3   Let's say your department needs another copier. You've no-
ticed that accounting has three machines, one of which is almost never used. The head of that department says it's okay to
take her extra copier, but the petty bureaucrat in charge of office equipment demands a long memo explaining in excruciat-
ing detail why you need it—with cc's to at least five other people who also have to give their approval, including the CEO,
who happens to be in Belgrade for the month and can't be
reached due to political upheaval.

4   How to cope? If you wait patiently, you'll be ready for retirement before the order comes through. Getting angry will
just make the petty bureaucrat gloat with satisfaction, because
frustrating others' wishes is her game.

5   There's only one way to deal with this type: You must be-
friend her. Remember: She's insecure, a lonely misfit, desperate for a kind word or smile, shunned because she's so self-
important and hateful. If you want that copier, start sucking
up. Ask her to lunch. Show an excessive interest in her
prize geraniums and philandering husband over your tuna
melt and you'll be whizzing through that pile by the end of
the day.

2. Credit Grabbers

6   In most cases, the thief is your boss, which puts you in a bind. Psychologist William Knaus, author of *Change Your Life Now*, says this is the problem Lee Iacocca* ran into with Henry Ford. "Iacocca talks about how threatened Ford was when he [Iacocca] started to get a lot of good publicity," Knaus explains. "Iacocca tried to make it work at Ford, but it was a losing proposition, because his credit-grabber boss was the most powerful person in the organization."

7   Eventually, Ford fired Iacocca, which was the best thing that ever happened to him—he went on to great success at Chrysler. "There are some people you simply shouldn't work for," Knaus asserts. "Life is too short to spend month after month, year after year, reporting to a parasitic boss who's going to damage your self-esteem."

8   If the culprit is a peer or subordinate, however, you have more options. The key is to document, document, document. After any meeting with a credit grabber, instantly send a memo to her and a copy to your boss, summarizing whatever ideas you contributed. If you team up on a project, create a computerized system outlining each of your responsibilities under the guise of getting organized. And keep quiet about any terrific ideas until they're documented as belonging to you.

3. Backstabber

9   Many backstabbers are what Michael Zey, M.D., author of *Winning With People*, calls friendly enemies. They're helpful and encouraging when you're down, he says, "but when you finally get that raise or promotion, they subtly start undermining your confidence and questioning your abilities." Even more insidious are those who remain friendly to your face and do their nasty work behind the scenes.

10   Rumormongering is their most common and malignant tactic. Rumors can be impossible to counter once they've been spread, but you can insulate yourself against them by developing a network of supportive colleagues who'll report all office gossip to you. If you know who the fiend is, enlist their help to defeat her by confronting her directly, spreading a counter-rumor, or reporting her to management.

*Lee Iacocca is a former CEO at Chrysler.

4. Nonstop Talkers

11   She plops down in your office, regardless of what you're doing at the moment, and launches into a litany of complaints about how the boss doesn't appreciate her; how she was overcharged when she took her incontinent dog, Spot, to the vet; how unfair it is that international terrorism is forcing her to wait in long lines at the airport. The usual signals, like saying, "I'm on deadline and can't talk now," don't deter her in the least.

12   Courtesy stops most of us from employing the kind of drastic tactics that actually work with this bulldozer. Recognize that divesting yourself of a motormouth may call for behavior your mother wouldn't approve of. First, try the kind of preemptive strike employed by media mogul Ted Turner. Turner tells people at the outset of a conversation how much time he can give them. When the allotted period has elapsed, he'll say something like "Your five minutes are up, and I've gotta go."

13   If that doesn't work, most experts agree that it's okay to employ even more abrupt measures. If she corners you at the water cooler, mumble an apology and take off in the opposite direction. If she has you trapped behind your desk, tell her you have to make a call, then pick up the phone and start talking very loudly. Even the most relentless blatherers will get the message eventually and start approaching colleagues who are nicer than you. You can bet your rude behavior will be at the top of their nonstop complaint list.

5. Alarmists

14   This corporate Chicken Little constantly races into your office with doomsday reports: You're getting a new boss who's so tyrannical he makes Attila the Hun* look like Leo Buscaglia†; such radical downsizing is on the way that the cleaning person will be doing your job. You have a panic attack every time you see this squawker coming down the hall.

15   Unfortunately, these days the sky really is falling on so many hardworking women that the office alarmist may be spreading an all-too-accurate message. Be smart and use her latest warning as a wake-up call. Think about what you'd do if you

---

*Attila the Hun was a violent barbarian of ancient Asia and Europe.
†Leo Buscaglia is a contemporary public relations expert.

did lose your job. Who would hire you? Do you have a network of contacts who'll help you? Talk to a few headhunters* and find out what's out there. Then, when the alarmist comes around, you can greet her latest disaster scenario by saying, "Who cares?"

6. Control Freaks

16   Control freaks are probably the most infuriating and hardest to handle of all difficult coworkers because they're so completely relentless. These obsessive-compulsives don't stop at a hands-on approach; they need to have a stranglehold on everything they touch. Your work is continually met with such comments as "Let's just check those figures one more time" and "I don't think that'll work; why don't we do it my way?" According to psychiatrist John M. Oldham, coauthor of *The New Personality Self Portrait: Why You Think, Work, Love, and Act the Way You Do*, control freaks "are tense, strained, anxious, and overwhelmed by the amount of work they have to do." Yet they're willing to devote so much time and energy to their jobs that they tend to move up in their professions, so chances are, you'll someday run into an overbearing higher-up.

17   According to psychologist Barry Lubetkin, of the Institute for Behavior Therapy in New York, passive resistance is the most effective way of dealing with these types. "Confrontation will only trigger even more controlling behavior," he says, "so avoid arguments and power struggles at all costs." When this coworker obsesses about some insignificant detail, make a neutral comment like "I understand what you're saying," then go about your business. He'll think you agreed with him and feel reassured.

7. Snoops

18   You can't leave a single piece of paper on your desk, because she always manages to read everything, personal and work-related. She grills you about your private life during business discussions, and you've even seen her lurking behind doorways while you chat with your boss.

19   Unlike backstabbers, who accumulate information to use against you, snoops have no ulterior motive; they just love to gossip. They're the kind of people for whom the saying "Get a life"

*Headhunters are people who find employees for companies.

was invented. The solution: Give them something to feed on without revealing personal secrets—so make stuff up! Leave hot fictional love notes from imaginary boyfriends on your desk. When she inquires about your personal life, tell her a lurid tale of multiple marriages and affairs with celebrities. When other colleagues come back to you asking if these stories are true, laugh and say, "I made all that up to get Mary Jane off my back."

8. Put-down Artist

20   "It took you a whole month to do this report."

21   "I can't believe they hired you with only a year's experience."

22   Verbal zingers act like sandpaper, rubbing slowly across your sense of self, eventually wearing it away. If you work for a put-down artist or with the kind of coworkers who constantly throw barbs your way, you'll soon dread coming into the office.

23   The first step in self-defense is acknowledging you've been hurt. Then set up a defense. Jennifer James, author of *Defending Yourself Against Criticism*, offers these strategies for countering an attack:

- Agree with everything the sniper says. This works with people who are so dense that nothing else gets to them or who have a sense of humor. For example:

  Put-down: "Are you sure you spoke with the sales department before using these figures? They don't look right to me."
  Defense: "Sales department? Why would I speak to them?"

- Register the hit. Say something like "Ooh, that really hurt," and go on with the conversation. This is a signal that you're not easy prey, and the tactic should stop everyone but the worst offenders.

- Send it back. For example:

  Put-down: "Are you sure you should be eating that doughnut?"
  Defense: "What I eat is a personal matter."

9. Bullies

24   Most of us adhere to an unspoken social contract that includes a modicum of considerate behavior. Bullies are unaware

that such an agreement exists. Their no-holds-barred tactics include public humiliation, making scenes, threatening to get you fired, and generally treating you like an unruly two-year-old instead of an adult.

25   Why do these outrageous tactics work? In his book *Coping With Difficult People,* psychologist Robert Bramson explains that bullies possess tremendous power because of the typical responses their behavior arouses in their victims: "confusion, mental or physical flight, a sense of helpless frustration that leads to tears or a tantrumlike rage." In other words, they get away with it because we let them.

26   The traditional wisdom about a schoolyard bully applies as well to the corporate type: You have to stand up to her. Bullies will often back down if you show you're willing to fight. Your strategy:

- Use positive body language. Don't let your shoulders droop and eyes drop when intimidated. Look her in the eye, and don't retreat.
- Give her time to cool down. "Remain in place and wait," recommends Bramson. "When the attack begins to lose momentum, jump in."
- Don't become paralyzed by fear. Even if you're so distraught you can't come up with the right retort, say something—anything to counter the onslaught.
- Stay rational. Ignore the intimidation, and slowly and reasonably make your case.

Exercise 2   Discussion and Critical Thinking

1. What is the main subject for the classification?

2. What is the principle, or basis, of the classification?

3. How many classes are there?

4. How would you rank the classes, starting with the most troublesome?

5. Why don't you tell the coworkers from hell to go back where
   they came from?

6. Which of the classes of coworkers can be identified most easily?

7. Which groups also exist in settings other than work-related on
   campus?

8. This passage has no conclusion. Should there be one? Explain
   why this form works or does not work for you.

✳ Reading-Related Writing

(See Classification, page 23, and Cause and Effect, page 21.)

"How to Deal with a Difficult Boss"

1. Write about one or more of the five types of bad bosses, giving examples from your own experience. (See Exemplification, page 18.)
2. Discuss one subdivision of the bully bosses (such as those who use
   words, threats of job loss, and threats of physical harm) and explain
   what they do, why they do it, and what kinds of damage they do.
3. Using this essay as a model, write a classification of good bosses.
4. Hogarty mentions that bad bosses are often made worse by bad
   employees. Write a classification of bad employees, perhaps
   from a good boss's perspective.
5. Using these traits from bad bosses, write about other people you
   have dealt with: bad teachers, preachers, cops, parents, siblings.

"Coworkers from Hell and How to Cope"

6. Write an essay about one or more annoying coworkers you have
   encountered. Explain how you coped. (See Exemplification, page
   18.)
7. Using this essay as a model, write about one or more fellow students, ride sharers, roommates, companions, or neighbors you
   have known and endured.
8. Using this essay as a model, write your own classification of enjoyable coworkers (or enjoyable people in another setting, such
   as fellow students, companions, ride sharers, and roommates).

9

Guns to Go

Some say guns are the principal cause of violence; others say guns could be the principal cause of peace. Few people are without an opinion on this subject.

In this chapter, we have a gun promoter and a gun abolitionist.

- "Letting Teachers Pack Guns Will Make America's Schools Safer" expands the educator's job description to something that once would have fit only the U.S. Marshall in a frontier showdown: "Out in the classroom, there is only one way to stop the killers and the spoilers, and that's with the heat-packin' guru and the smell of gunsmoke."
- "Get a Knife, Get a Dog, But Get Rid of Guns" is a disarming article asking readers to check their guns in at the toxic-products section of the community dump.

Letting Teachers Pack Guns Will Make America's Schools Safer

John R. Lott Jr.

John R. Lott Jr., a resident scholar at the American Enterprise Institute, is the author of The Bias Against Guns *(Regnery, 2003). This article was first published in the* Los Angeles Times *in 2004.*

1   Banning guns from schools seems the obvious way to keep children safe. Utah, though, is doing the opposite, and is stirring up debate across the nation.

2   Acting under a new state law, school districts across Utah have started drawing up regulations allowing teachers and other public employees to carry concealed guns on school property. Opponents are still trying to fight the law, and at first glance their concern about firearms in schools is understandable. Last Sunday in New Jersey, an attack by armed teenagers against three fellow students and randomly chosen townspeople was narrowly averted.

109

3   But that's not the whole picture. Consider an analogy: Suppose a criminal is stalking you or your family. Would you feel safe putting a sign in front of your home saying, "This Home Is a Gun-Free Zone"? Law-abiding citizens might be pleased by such a sign, but to criminals it would be an invitation.

4   In 1985, just eight states had right-to-carry laws—laws that automatically grant permits for concealed weapons once applicants pass a criminal background check, pay their fees and when required, complete a training class. Today, 35 states do.

5   Examining all the multiple-victim public shootings in the United States from 1977 to 1999 shows that on average, states that adopt right-to-carry laws experience a 60% drop in the rates at which the attacks occur, and a 78% drop in the rates at which people are killed or injured from such attacks.

6   To the extent such attacks still occurred in right-to-carry states, they overwhelmingly take place in so-called "gun-free zones." Indeed, the attack last week in Meridian, Mississippi, in which five people were killed took place in a Lockheed Martin plant where employees were forbidden to have guns.

7   The effect of right-to-carry laws is greater on multiple-victim public shootings than on other crimes for a simple reason: Increasing the probability that someone will be able to protect himself improves deterrence. Though it may be statistically unlikely that any single person in a crowd is carrying a concealed handgun, the probability that at least one person is armed is high.

8   Contrary to many people's impressions, before the federal law was enacted in 1995 it was possible for teachers and other adults with concealed-handgun permits to carry guns on school property in many states.

9   Many of the concerns about accidents and other problems are unwarranted. The real problems at schools occurred only after the ban. The rash of student shootings at schools began in October 1997 in Pearl, Mississippi.

10   Public reaction against guns is understandable, given the horrific events shown on TV. But the more than 2 million times each year that Americans use guns defensively are never discussed. In more than 90% of those cases, simply brandishing a weapon is sufficient to cause a criminal to break off an attack. My research also shows that citizens with guns helped stop about a third of the post-1997 public school shootings, stepping in before uniformed police could arrive.

11   Last year, news broadcasts on the three main TV networks carried about 190,000 words on gun crime stories. Not one segment featured a civilian using a gun to stop a crime. Newspapers are not much better.

12   Police are extremely important in deterring crime, but they almost always arrive after the crime has been committed. Annual surveys of crime victims in the United States by the Justice Department show that when confronted by a criminal, people are safest if they have a gun.

13   Just as the threat of arrest and prison can deter criminals, so can the fact that victims can defend themselves.

14   For multiple-victim shootings, the biggest factor determining the amount of harm is the length of time between when an attack starts and when someone with a gun can stop the attack. The longer the delay, the more are harmed.

15   Good intentions do not necessarily make good laws. What counts is whether the laws ultimately save lives. Unfortunately, too many gun laws primarily disarm law-abiding citizens, not criminals.

Exercise 1   Discussion and Critical Thinking

1. In paragraph 3, Lott presents an analogy about a house posted as a gun-free zone. The opposite would be a gun-holding zone. Do you think Lott would prefer that schools be posted to indicate that educators are carrying firearms to deter potential troublemakers? How would you feel about that posting?

2. Lott mentions that the victims at the Meridian, Mississippi, firm were forbidden to have guns. Would you feel more or less secure if you knew that your fellow workers, or perhaps your adult fellow students at college, were carrying concealed firearms?

3. In paragraphs 9 through 11, Lott offers an abundance of support for his view. As a critical thinker, what questions should you ask about his use of statistics and reasoning?

Get a Knife, Get a Dog, But Get Rid of Guns

Molly Ivins

> *A nationally syndicated newspaper columnist, essayist, book au-*
> *thor, and occasional radio and television commentator, Molly*
> *Ivins, according to the* Houston Press, *"leaves . . . no sacred cow*
> *unbarbequed." The* Texas Observer *says, "Seamless . . . Ivins has*
> *shown herself to be not just a journalist who knows how to drawl*
> *but a populist stylist, fashioning a vernacular that blends the*
> *high, the low, and the Lone-Staresque, preaching and irony,*
> *Shakespeare and sumbitches." Her books include* Molly Ivins
> Can't Say That, Can She? *(1992),* Nothin' But Good Times Ahead
> *(1994), and* You Got to Dance with Them What Brung You *(1999).*

1   Guns. Everywhere guns.

2   Let me start this discussion by pointing out that I am not antigun. I'm pro-knife. Consider the merits of the knife.

3   In the first place, you have to catch up with someone in order to stab him. A general substitution of knives for guns would promote physical fitness. We'd turn into a whole nation of great runners. Plus, knives don't ricochet. And people are seldom killed while cleaning their knives.

4   As a civil libertarian, I, of course, support the Second Amendment. And I believe it means exactly what it says:

5   *A well-regulated militia being necessary to the security of a free state, the right of the people to keep and bear arms shall not be infringed.* Fourteen-year-old boys are not part of a well-regulated militia. Members of wacky religious cults are not part of a well-regulated militia. Permitting unregulated citizens to have guns is destroying the security of this free state.

6   I am intrigued by the arguments of those who claim to follow the judicial doctrine of original intent. How do they know it was the dearest wish of Thomas Jefferson's heart that teenage drug dealers should cruise the cities of this nation perforating their fellow citizens with assault rifles? Channeling?

7   There is more hooey spread about the Second Amendment. It says quite clearly that guns are for those who form part of a well-regulated militia, that is, the armed forces, including the National Guard. Their reasons for keeping them away from everyone else get clearer by the day.

8   The comparison most often used is that of the automobile, another lethal object that is regularly used to wreak great carnage. Obviously, this society is full of people who haven't

enough common sense to use an automobile properly. But we haven't outlawed cars yet.

9   We do, however, license them and their owners, restrict their use to presumably sane and sober adults, and keep track of who sells them to whom. At a minimum, we should do the same with guns.

10   In truth, there is no rational argument for guns in this society. This is no longer a frontier nation in which people hunt their own food. It is a crowded, overwhelmingly urban country in which letting people have access to guns is a continuing disaster. Those who want guns—whether for target shooting, hunting, or potting rattlesnakes (get a hoe)—should be subject to the same restrictions placed on gun owners in England, a nation in which liberty has survived nicely without an armed populace.

11   The argument that "guns don't kill people" is patent nonsense. Anyone who has ever worked in a cop shop knows how many family arguments end in murder because there was a gun in the house. Did the gun kill someone? No. But if there had been no gun, no one would have died. At least not without a good foot race first. Guns do kill. Unlike cars, that is all they do.

12   Michael Crichton makes an interesting argument about technology in his thriller *Jurassic Park*. He points out that power without discipline is making this society into a wreckage. By the time someone who studies the martial arts becomes a master—literally able to kill with bare hands—that person has also undergone years of training and discipline. But any fool can pick up a gun and kill with it.

13   "A well-regulated militia" surely implies both long training and long discipline. That is the least, the very least, that should be required of those who are permitted to have guns, because a gun is literally the power to kill. For years I used to enjoy taunting my gun-nut friends about their psychosexual hang-ups— always in a spirit of good cheer, you understand. But letting the noisy minority in the NRA force us to allow this carnage to continue is just plain insane.

14   I do think gun nuts have a power hang-up. I don't know what is missing in their psyches that they need to feel they have the power to kill. But no sane society would allow this to continue.

15   Ban the damn things. Ban them all.

16   You want protection? Get a dog.

Exercise 2 Discussion and Critical Thinking

1. **Tone** is the way an author addresses his or her reader and subject—playfully, scornfully, seriously, comically, overbearingly, angrily, submissively, ironically. Why does Ivins use humor in paragraphs 2 and 3, saying that she is "pro-knife" and that the substitution of knives for guns would "promote physical fitness"?

2. **Refutation** is the presentation of the opposing view and its fundamental inadequacy. It is sometimes omitted. Ivins takes the other tack. She builds her essay around refutations. Why do you think she uses that approach? Does it have something to do with the emotional background of this issue?

3. Ivins attacks five specific points in her essay. Some of the points are only implied because Ivins expects her audience to be familiar with the often articulated pro-gun position. Write a one-sentence statement of each view she believes pro-gun advocates hold.

   Paragraph 5: The pro-gun advocates would say, _____

   _____

   Paragraph 6: The pro-gun advocates would say, _____

   _____

   Paragraph 8: The pro-gun advocates would say,_____

   _____

   Paragraph 11: The pro-gun advocates would say,_____

   _____

   Paragraph 12: The pro-gun advocates would say,_____

   _____

4. Of the five points stated in the preceeding item, has Ivins been fair in her implications?

5. What does Ivins gain by mixing slang terms, such as "wacky" (paragraph 5), "hooey" (paragraph 7), and "gun-nut" (paragraph 13), with standard phrasing?

6. What is the stylistic effect of the first sentence and the last two? Why do they gain special attention?

✳ Reading-Related Writing

(See Argument, page 28.)

"Letting Teachers Pack Guns Will Make America's Schools Safer"

1. Write an essay in which you generally agree or disagree with Lott. (See Analysis by Division, page 18.)
2. Write a two-part summary-and-reaction response to Lott's essay. Keep in mind that the summary gives the main points and the reaction is your view of the work. (See pages 7–8.)
3. Evaluate Lott's essay for writing techniques and especially for logic. (See Argument, page 28.)

"Get a Knife, Get a Dog, But Get Rid of Guns"

4. Write an essay in which you generally agree or disagree with Ivins. (See Analysis by Division, page 18.)
5. Write a two-part summary-and-reaction response to Ivins's essay. Keep in mind that the summary gives the main points and the reaction is your view of the work. (See pages 6–7.)
6. Evaluate Ivins's essay for writing techniques and especially for logic.
7. Compare and contrast the views of Lott with those of Ivins. Your main intention may be just to show that the two have polar differences or that one is superior to the other in terms of logic and your values. (See Comparison and Contrast, page 24.)

10

Rocking Chair Rhapsodies
and Blues

You've heard the charge: What're we going to do with the older generation? They're driving recklessly, popping Viagra like jellybeans, scooping up jobs in McDonald's, forming political action groups, and playing Bingo till the sun comes up. Those are the wild and wacky hyperactive geriatrics.

Many others have traded in their automobiles and shopping carts for wheelchairs and walkers, cruising corridors of nursing homes, living desperate oatmeal lives in a fog of ammonia. A remarkable number have sustained their dignity in their own homes or those of family, often against great odds and trends.

Three readings give different perspectives on old age:

- "Ultimate Recycling: Adopt an Elder" suggests that oldsters can be put to good use: Childless couples could save bucks and bother by adopting old people instead of kids.
- "Tamales, a Family Production" shows a matriarch contentedly directing three generations in an ageless tradition.
- "Though Blindness Came to Grandpa, He Could See" is a ballad about an old man who lost his sight but gamely refused to relinquish his world.

Ultimate Recycling: Adopt an Elder

Heather Cash

> *Heather Cash, a sixteen-year-old college freshman, read Jonathan Swift's satirical essay "A Modest Proposal" and set out to write her own about an issue that concerned her: treatment of the elderly. If you have not read Swift's work, just sign on to the Internet to a search engine such as Google and key in the title and author. Reading "A Modest Proposal" will add another dimension to the wonderfully witty essay by Cash.*

1   Every year, childless couples in the United States shell out millions of dollars, investing in fertility pills, ovulation calculators, specialists, egg donors, sperm banks, surrogate mothers, adoption agencies, and even books showing alternative methods and positions supposedly best suited to help couples conceive. It's heartbreaking to think that even with modern technology, it is still impossible for some couples to bring their own children into the world or to obtain others. These couples are repeatedly left disappointed and frustrated, still yearning for someone of their own to take care of. It is indeed unfortunate that so many have yet to discover an untapped resource that may be just around the corner, that would most likely fill the void so many wannabe-mommies-and-daddies feel—nursing homes.

2   Many people do not realize it, but with the exception of size, the nursing home elderly are just like babies. The majority of old folks cannot walk independently or feed themselves, are bedridden, and have diapers, just like babies. Like babies, most old people, and I mean ninety-plus, are completely helpless. Both babies and these elderly have few to no teeth. Both receive special movie theater and bus discounts. Restaurants often supply special menus and services for people on both sides of the age extremes. Different government programs are specifically designed to cater to both their medical and their housing needs. One way in which the old may differ from babies is old people are in abundance all over the United States; no matter where you live, you are sure to find an old person or two who are perfect for any family.

3   While the old and young may be very similar in and of themselves, the two are very different when it comes to sharing your home. Adopting an elderly person instead of having a baby may prove to actually be better than raising a child. When a couple has a child, they are always taking a gamble. There is no assurance that little Bobby or Susie will turn out just the way their parents wanted them to. With Grandpa Henry and Grandma Mabel, what you see is what you get. Unlike children, an old person will not bring up embarrassing stories or facts about your family to guests, because they will not remember them, and if by some chance unwanted words are spoken, they can easily be dismissed by stating, "They're senile." In any case, who isn't aware of how little attention is paid to what old people say? Old people are much easier to keep track of than the

young. They are too slow to get lost at the mall or theme parks, and it's guaranteed that someone with an old person will never have to go through the hassle of chasing Grandma Mabel all over a supermarket. She will never drop to the floor and have a temper tantrum, because she knows she can't get up. It's much easier to break a promise to Grandpa Henry than to little Bobby. Say Bobby wants to go to Disneyland. I bet Bobby will not stop yapping at you until he has been to this so-called "happiest place on earth." On the other hand, Grandpa Henry is easier to trick. Say he's dying to go to the doctor, his request can be effortlessly set aside with, "Don't you remember? We went yesterday." Old folks will almost certainly accept that answer, whereas no child would ever buy that.

4   No expensive toys, computers, video-game consoles, or eventually cars, are ever needed for the elderly, Grandpa Henry and Grandma Mabel both grew up during the Depression and they are tightwads anyway, so just set up a television that's always tuned to the Game Show Network in the living room and they are set.

5   Perhaps you will win the old-person lottery, and adopt Grandma Beatrice who's been hoarding money under her mattress since the 1930s. Grandma Beatrice, no doubt, will reward you for your kindheartedness and leave you to inherit all of her worldly assets, provided you take a little initiative, have a little persistence, and keep a close eye when you hire a "lawyer" to help her with her will. Ever feel like you need a time out from Grandma Mabel? Why not send her to stay out in the shed for a while? The elderly have gotten used to living in such conditions, she won't mind, and that way she can guard the tools from would-be burglars. You don't have to worry about inviting some teenager from your neighborhood to come to your house on Saturday night to watch Granny. You can go out to the movies guilt free. In fact, with the elderly, there are also no worries about college tuition or future undesirable in-laws. It's very unlikely they will ever request a loan. With little Bobby or Susie, it's impossible to determine how long you will be required to help him or her out; Grandma Mabel and Grandpa Henry have a life expectancy that is likely to rid you of any obligation society feels you owe them. Also, old people can be made to do chores! If you don't mind how long it takes for the yard to be cleaned, just hand the rake to reliable old Grandpa Henry. He probably has a

great deal of yard-work experience from his youth. With all this information, it's a surprise why more people have not decided to adopt an old person of their own.

6   Here is another great idea. Don't have plans for the weekend? Why not invite a couple of friends over and hide Grandpa Henry's dentures and glasses? There is nothing more hilarious than watching a feeble old man scurry about trying to maintain a semblance of self-respect, while toppling over his wheelchair and knocking down all his meds. Also, it's great to dress Grandma Mabel and Grandpa Henry up in crazy clothes and even cut and style their hair. Don't worry, they will go along with it, they will be more than happy to receive the attention. Why not share the fun and send a few snapshots to their biological children, who probably long to spend time with their parents but are rendered unable to because of the stringent demands of modern life?

7   Adopting an old person is a benefit to the state as well. It relieves taxpayers and the government of spending money to fund services for the old, which are often inadequate. A person does not have to go far to find horror stories about the deplorable conditions of nursing homes and medical care for the elderly. Adopting an elderly person will definitely give you bragging rights about doing your part for charity. I'm sure when this movement takes full force you can expect some sort of tax write-off from the government. If you are religious, you can be certain this act of kindness will lead to a good word being passed on to the man above, even before you arrive at the pearly gates. Many old people have various hobbies they have acquired from past skill-related jobs like sewing, knitting, or other forms of craftsmanship. Perhaps, some of these handcrafted treasures could be sold to help supplement the money you may need to spend on your adopted old person. If you are in need of making a little extra money on the side, many of the medications prescribed to Grandma Mabel are in high demand; they can easily be resold and distributed by your friendly local "street pharmacist."

8   One of the biggest benefits of adopting an old person is that you are actually investing in your own future. Eventually, most of us reach old age. Hopefully by starting this trend, when time renders you in the same position of your adopted old person, someone will adopt you. So make sure to invite your friends and family to your home to share the joy on adoption day, and celebrate the old person's birthday every year. It isn't difficult to

see that American society devalues the old. It's no wonder why so many adults choose to push aside the people who brought them into this world and took care of them throughout their childhood, instead of respecting them. Why raise a child who will cost you an immense amount of money, time, and stress, and may eventually abandon you at some decrepit retirement home? At least when this old person leaves you, you can be sure it was unavoidable, and not because they resent you and are unwilling to sacrifice a little of their own finances or time to take care of you.

Exercise 1   Discussion and Critical Thinking

1. What pattern of writing does Cash use for the design of her essay?

2. How might this be called an argument at two levels?

3. **Satire** is a way of writing that holds up an idea to ridicule. Use paragraph numbers to identify ideas that are satirical.

4. What hypothetical (supposed) examples are most effective?

Tamales, a Family Production

Lvette Lohayza

> *Student Lvette Lohayza wrote her simple personal essay in response to this assignment:*
>
> > *Write an essay about how to do something or about how something was done. For example, you might write about how your family cooks and serves a special holiday meal. Placed within a cultural framework, it could interestingly provide information about both the process and the culture, blending the two.*

1   Christmas Eve at Grandma's house is a joyous time, especially for the females of my family. That is the time when we assist Grandma in making her wonderfully palatable tamales. Beginning at daybreak and ending after darkness, it is an occa-

sion of bonding and reunion. Grandma always greets us with a freshly brewed pot of coffee and some *dulce.* The next eight hours will be a whirlwind of lively talk and cooperative work.

2   Soon after our coffee, we drive off to a special market called the *mercado,* where Grandma leads us in shopping for the items we need. First, we visit the butcher, whose name is Pepé. He is awaiting Grandma's arrival, as he does every year. He has put aside his freshest beefsteaks just for her. She carefully chooses the reddest and the most visibly fat-free meat available. According to Grandma, the meat must be bright red because that is a clear indication of its freshness, and freshness is especially what her tamales depend on. Next, we follow Grandma to an aisle where she examines piles of *ojas,* or corn husks, which are used for wrapping and cooking the tamales. We help her select and count out an equal number of large and medium husks. Then we stop at the canned-food section for what is known as *chili de las palmas,* a hot and spicy red sauce. Finally, we reach the section of the market that prepares and sells *masa,* a cornmeal substance for encasing the meat in the tamales. Shopping as a group has brought us closer together and reminded us of the complete annual event, which will now include the cooking and later will end at the dinner table.

3   As soon as we return, at nearly eight in the morning, Grandma, like a colonel, delegates duties for the first stage of our work. A veteran crew boils the meat in black cast-iron pots, each large piece with a clove of garlic embedded in it for flavor. Several older women sort out the corn husks, large from medium, as the younger girls wash them and put them in separate stacks to dry on a six-foot table. By the time the husks have dried, the boiled meat is ready for shredding. With Grandma watching over our shoulders, the room is full of laughter and talk and enjoyable industry. Grandma herself sets two twenty-five-gallon shining steel pots onto burners and pours in about four inches of water. Then she drops in racks that will be used for steaming the tamales. Meanwhile, as the spicy aroma fills the kitchen, and the ambiance becomes ever more cheerful, we all gather around the table and shred the meat with our bare hands.

4   After the meat has been shredded, we mix it with chili sauce and olives and begin forming the tamales on the large table, where the dry corn husks lie in stacks of medium and large. The first step is to use a butter knife to spread *masa* on a large corn husk. Next, we fork a couple of heaps of meat onto

the *masa*. Then we add another generous layer of *masa* and cap it with a medium corn husk. Carefully, we roll the edges of the larger leaf over the edges of the medium leaf to seal the tamale so that no meat or *masa* leaks out while cooking. This continual spreading, stuffing, and rolling of the tamales will go on for the next two to three hours.

5   Once all of the tamales have been rolled, they are carefully stacked in the large cooking pots and a wet hand towel is placed on top of the tamales to trap the steam while they are cooking. Four to six hours of steam-cooking pass before the tamales are ready for consumption.

6   By this time, we all have insatiable appetites and are ready for this well-deserved meal. Smiling broadly and listening to compliments as she takes orders, meaning requests, Grandma is the main server. The children, who have been peeking into the kitchen and begging for bites, are served at their own table. Standing in line with plates, the men are calling out the numbers of tamales they need to satisfy their prodigious appetites. The young men, who are, in their own way, part of the group effort because they provided valet parking as families arrived, follow their fathers and uncles in line. We females, independent as some of us may be most of the year, are fortunate in that we get to enjoy the whole process as team members with Grandma and family, and for that experience, the eating of the Christmas tamales is all the better.

Exercise 2   Discussion and Critical Thinking

1. This essay explains how something is done; therefore, it is a process analysis (see page 20). What preparations are made before the process can begin and what steps are followed in preparing the meal? Use the following outline for your answer.

   I. Preparation
      A.
      B.
      C.
   II. Steps
      A.
      B.
      C.
      D.

2. Explain how the grandmother is an integral part of the family.

3. Explain how the whole family is involved.

Though Blindness Came to Grandpa, He Could See

John Cordell

> *Freelance author John Cordell had a very special grandfather. In his late seventies, Cordell's grandfather became blind. It was a gradual process, and the old man refused to give up his active life on his farm. He came up with a plan. He would string wires over his head and run them from his home to parts of his farm: the barn, the hen house, the orchard, the garden, the mailbox, and, of course, the outhouse. After he became blind, Cordell's grandfather would attach a strap and ring to the appropriate wire and make his way "like a bat on the wing" to his destination.*
>
> *The ballad can be sung to the melody of Grandpa's favorite hymn, "When the Roll Is Called Up Yonder."*

Map for Grandpa's World

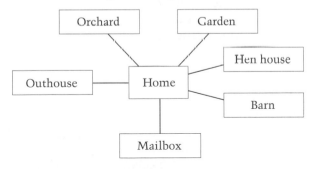

One day for him the sun it set,
Then he could see no more,
And Grandpa took his blindness as a sign.
He believed the Lord had struck his eyes
5   To take his sight away,
'Cause he'd strayed from the straight and narrow line.

He said, "Don't move my furniture,
And don't lead me around,
Watch out when I come walkin' with my cane.

10 I'll give you hugs and touch your face,
   I'll listen to you well,
   I've still got four senses and a brain."

Chorus:
   Though blindness came to Grandpa,
   Though blindness came to Grandpa,
15 Though blindness came to Grandpa,
   Though blindness came to Grandpa,
   He could see.

   "String some wires above my head
   And all across my farm,
20 And add on a holdin' strap and ring.
   That will give me guidelines
   For where I need to go,
   Through the darkness like a bat on the wing."

   The wires were black highways
25 On his road map for the blind,
   Goin' to the barnyard and to the fields of grain.
   They took him to the mailbox,
   For the words he couldn't read,
   They took him through the sunshine and the rain.

Chorus

30 He could see with his fingers,
   He could see with his ears,
   And his intuition would ring true.
   He saw all his life of wonders,
   With its pleasures and its pains,
35 Just a wise man with a different point of view.

Chorus

Exercise 3 Discussion and Critical Thinking

1. You could call Grandpa's behavior courageous. Could you also
   call it heroic? Explain.

2. Fill in the blanks to show how this ballad is a narrative (see Narration, page 15), or story.

Situation:

Conflict:

Struggle:

Result:

Meaning:

✳ Reading-Related Writing

"Ultimate Recycling: Adopt an Elder"

1. Using Cash's essay (or if you have read "A Modest Proposal" by Jonathan Swift, use his) as a model, write your own satirical essay on a topic of concern to you.
2. Write an evaluation of Cash's essay. How effective is it? Refer to details, phrasing, and organization. (See Analysis by Division, page 18.)

"Tamales, a Family Production"

3. Write about an elderly family member who is actively and constructively involved in family matters. The activity may be cooking, building, repairing, growing, or maintaining something. Explain how the involvement occurs. (See Process Analysis, page 20.)

"Though Blindness Came to Grandpa, He Could See"

4. Rewrite this ballad in sentences so that it appears as a regular story with the traditional story parts: situation, conflict, struggle, outcome, meaning. (See Narration, page 15.)
5. Write about an older person you know who has, within the confines of his or her life, been courageous in dealing with a significant problem: illness, disease, impairment (blindness, deafness, physical weakness or paralysis, emphysema), death in the family, family disgrace, or financial failure. (See Narration, page 15.)

11

Changing (Gender) Places

According to an old saw, you can't understand others without having walked a mile in their shoes (boots, moccasins). Perhaps it would be instructive if we were to apply that saying to gender matters, acknowledging that you can't understand the people of the other gender unless you have walked a mile in their shoes (dirty old sneakers, patent-leather pumps). That's what this chapter is about—walking in others' footwear, figuratively speaking.

Two essays will prepare you for an almost mission-impossible essay assignment exploring the hidden biases and stereotypes of your opposite gender.

- "Men Are from Mars, Women Are from Venus" explains the figurative planetary origins of males and females.
- "The Opposite Sex" is an account of one professor's efforts to take students to the opposite gender barrier and beyond.

Men Are from Mars, Women Are from Venus

John Gray

> *As a writer, marriage counselor, and seminar leader, John Gray specializes in understanding and dealing with gender difference. This excerpt comes from his best-selling book* Men Are from Mars, Women Are from Venus *(1992), in which he says men and women are so different they might as well have come from different planets. Like all generalizations, his don't perfectly fit all individuals within groups (genders), but he provides much for you to consider.*

1   The most frequently expressed complaint women have about men is that men don't listen. Either a man completely ignores [a woman] when she speaks to him, or he listens for a few beats, assesses what is bothering her, and then proudly puts on his Mr. Fix-It cap and offers her a solution to make her feel better. He is confused when she doesn't appreciate this gesture of love. No matter how many times she tells him that he's

not listening, he doesn't get it and keeps doing the same thing. She wants empathy, but he thinks she wants solutions.

2   The most frequently expressed complaint men have about women is that women are always trying to change them. When a woman loves a man she feels responsible to assist him in growing and tries to help him improve the way he does things. She forms a home-improvement committee, and he becomes her primary focus. No matter how much he resists her help, she persists—waiting for any opportunity to help him or tell him what to do. She thinks she's nurturing him, while he feels he's being controlled. Instead, he wants her acceptance.

3   These two problems can finally be solved by first under-standing why men offer solutions and why women seek to im-prove. Let's pretend to go back in time, where by observing life on Mars and Venus—before the planets discovered one another or came to Earth—we can gain some insights into men and women.

4   Martians value power, competency, efficiency, and achieve-ment. They are always doing things to prove themselves and de-velop their power and skills. Their sense of self is defined through their ability to achieve results. They experience fulfill-ment primarily through success and accomplishment.

5   Everything on Mars is a reflection of these values. Even their dress is designed to reflect their skills and competence. Police officers, soldiers, businessmen, scientists, cab drivers, technicians, and chefs all wear uniforms or at least hats to re-flect their competence and power.

6   They don't read magazines like *Psychology Today*, *Self*, or *People*. They are more concerned with outdoor activities, like hunting, fishing, and racing cars. They are interested in the news, weather, and sports and couldn't care less about romance novels and self-help books.

7   They are more interested in "objects" and "things" rather than people and feelings. Even today on Earth, while women fan-tasize about romance, men fantasize about powerful cars, faster computers, gadgets, gizmos, and new more powerful technology. Men are preoccupied with the "things" that can help them ex-press power by creating results and achieving their goals.

8   Achieving goals is very important to a Martian because it is a way for him to prove his competence and thus feel good about himself. And for him to feel good about himself he must

achieve these goals by himself. Someone else can't achieve them for him. Martians pride themselves on doing things all by themselves. Autonomy is a symbol of efficiency, power, and competence.

9   Understanding this Martian characteristic can help women understand why men resist so much being corrected or being told what to do. To offer a man unsolicited advice is to presume that he doesn't know what to do or that he can't do it on his own. Men are very touchy about this, because the issue of competence is so very important to them.

10   Because he is handling his problems on his own, a Martian rarely talks about his problems unless he needs expert advice. He reasons: "Why involve someone else when I can do it by myself?" He keeps his problems to himself unless he requires help from another to find a solution. Asking for help when you can do it yourself is perceived as a sign of weakness.

11   However, if he truly does need help, then it is a sign of wisdom to get it. In this case, he will find someone he respects and then talk about his problem. Talking about a problem on Mars is an invitation for advice. Another Martian feels honored by the opportunity. Automatically he puts on his Mr. Fix-It hat, listens for a while, and then offers some jewels of advice.

12   This Martian custom is one of the reasons men instinctively offer solutions when women talk about problems. When a woman innocently shares upset feelings or explores out loud the problems of her day, a man mistakenly assumes she is looking for some expert advice. He puts on his Mr. Fix-It hat and begins giving advice; this is his way of showing love and of trying to help.

13   He wants to help her feel better by solving her problems. He wants to be useful to her. He feels he can be valued and thus worthy of her love when his abilities are used to solve her problems.

14   Once he has offered a solution, however, and she continues to be upset it becomes increasingly difficult for him to listen because his solution is being rejected and he feels increasingly useless.

15   He has no idea that by just listening with empathy and interest he can be supportive. He does not know that on Venus talking about problems is not an invitation to offer a solution.

16   Venusians have different values. They value love, communication, beauty, and relationships. They spend a lot of time

supporting, helping, and nurturing one another. Their sense of self is defined through their feelings and the quality of their relationships. They experience fulfillment through sharing and relating.

17   Everything on Venus reflects these values. Rather than building highways and tall buildings, the Venusians are more concerned with living together in harmony, community, and loving cooperation. Relationships are more important than work and technology. In most ways their world is the opposite of Mars.

18   They do not wear uniforms like the Martians (to reveal their competence). On the contrary, they enjoy wearing a different outfit every day, according to how they are feeling. Personal expression, especially of their feelings, is very important. They may even change outfits several times a day as their mood changes.

19   Communication is of primary importance. To share their personal feelings is much more important than achieving goals and success. Talking and relating to one another is a source of tremendous fulfillment.

20   This is hard for a man to comprehend. He can come close to understanding a woman's experience of sharing and relating by comparing it to the satisfaction he feels when he wins a race, achieves a goal, or solves a problem.

21   Instead of being goal oriented, women are relationship oriented; they are more concerned with expressing their goodness, love, and caring. Two Martians go to lunch to discuss a project or business goal; they have a problem to solve. In addition, Martians view going to a restaurant as an efficient way to approach food: no shopping, no cooking, and no washing dishes. For Venusians, going to lunch is an opportunity to nurture a relationship, for both giving support to and receiving support from a friend. Women's restaurant talk can be very open and intimate, almost like the dialogue that occurs between therapist and patient.

22   On Venus, everyone studies psychology and has at least a master's degree in counseling. They are very involved in personal growth, spirituality, and everything that can nurture life, healing, and growth. Venus is covered with parks, organic gardens, shopping centers, and restaurants.

23   Venusians are very intuitive. They have developed this ability through centuries of anticipating the needs of others.

They pride themselves on being considerate of the needs and feelings of others. A sign of great love is to offer help and assistance to another Venusian without being asked.

24   Because proving one's competence is not as important to a Venusian, offering help is not offensive, and needing help is not a sign of weakness. A man, however, may feel offended because when a woman offers advice he doesn't feel she trusts his ability to do it himself.

25   A woman has no conception of this male sensitivity because for her it is another feather in her hat if someone offers to help her. It makes her feel loved and cherished. But offering help to a man can make him feel incompetent, weak, and even unloved.

26   On Venus it is a sign of caring to give advice and suggestions. Venusians firmly believe that when something is working it can always work better. Their nature is to want to improve things. When they care about someone, they freely point out what can be improved and suggest how to do it. Offering advice and constructive criticism is an act of love.

27   Mars is very different. Martians are more solution oriented. If something is working, their motto is don't change it. Their instinct is to leave it alone if it is working. "Don't fix it unless it is broken" is a common expression.

28   When a woman tries to improve a man, he feels she is trying to fix him. He receives the message that he is broken. She doesn't realize her caring attempts to help him may humiliate him. She mistakenly thinks she is just helping him to grow.

Exercise 1 Discussion and Critical Thinking

1. Is Gray serious about his insights? What in this excerpt indicates his intention?

2. Does Gray oversimplify gender differences? Explain.

3. Do his views apply equally to different income and social classes?

4. How do styles in communication affect multiple areas of relationships—values, careers, friendships, activities, family, and so on?

5. Do the people you know fit into these behavioral patterns detailed by Gray?

6. Is he suggesting that men and women should break out of their patterns of thinking and behaving? Explain.

The Opposite Sex

Steven Doloff

Careers as professor of English and freelance writer merge in this essay by Steven Doloff. His subject is the circumstances of an original writing assignment he gave to his college students, one in which he asked them to address their preconceptions about gender roles. The article was first published in The Washington Post.

1   Having seen Dustin Hoffman's female impersonation in the movie *Tootsie,* I decided to give myself some reading over the Christmas recess by assigning in-class essays to my English composition students on how each would spend a day as a member of his or her respective opposite sex. From four classes I received approximately 100 essays. The sample, perhaps like the movie, proved both entertaining and annoying in its predictability.

2   The female students, as a group, took to the subject immediately and with obvious gusto, while the male students tended to wait a while (in several cases half the period), in something of a daze, before starting. The activities hypothetically engaged in by the women, whose ages averaged about 20, generally reflected two areas: envy of men's physical and social privileges, and curiosity regarding men's true feelings concerning women.

3   In their essays, women jauntily went places *alone,* and sometimes stayed out *all night.* They threw their clothes on the floor and left dishes in the sink. They hung out on the street and sweated happily in a variety of sports from football to weightlifting.

4   More than a third of them went out to cruise for dates. Appointing themselves in brand names of men's clothing and

dousing themselves in men's cologne I have never heard of (I was instructed to read *Gentleman's Quarterly* magazine), they deliberately and aggressively accosted women, *many* women, on the street, in discos, in supermarkets. Others sought out the proverbial locker room for the kinds of bull sessions they hoped would reveal the real nitty-gritty masculine mind at work (on the subject of women).

5   At least two female students in each class spent chunks of their essays under the sheets with imaginary girlfriends, wives or strangers, finding out with a kind of scientific zeal what sex is like as a man.

6   Some, but not all of the women ended their essays with a formal, almost obligatory sounding statement of preference to be a female, and of gratitude in returning to their correct gender after a day as Mr. Hyde.

7   The male students, after their initial paralysis wore off, did not write as much as the females. They seemed envious of very little that was female, and curious about nothing. Three or four spent their day as women frantically seeking medical help to turn back into men more quickly. Those who accepted the assignment more seriously, if unenthusiastically, either stayed home and apathetically checked off a list of domestic chores or, more evasively, went off to work in an office and engaged in totally asexual business office routines.

8   A small percentage of the men ventured into the more feminine pursuits of putting on makeup and going to the beauty parlor. They agreed looking good was important.

9   If they stayed home as housewives, when their hypothetical husbands returned from work they ate dinner, watched some television and then went right to sleep. If they were businesswomen, they came directly home after work, ate some dinner, watched TV and went right to sleep. A handful actually went out on dates, had dinner in the most expensive restaurants they could cajole their escorts into taking them to, and then, after being taken home, very politely slammed the doors in their escorts' faces and went right to sleep. Not one male student let anybody lay a finger on him/her.

10   Finally, the sense of heartfelt relief at the end of the male students' essays, underscored by the much-repeated fervent anticipation of masculinity returning with the dawn, seemed equivalent to that of jumping up after having been forced to sit on a lit stove.

11   Granted, my flimsy statistical sample is nothing to go to

the Ford Foundation with for research money. But on the other hand, do I really need to prove that young people even now are still burdened with sexist stereotypes and sexist self-images not nearly as vestigial as we would like to think? (One male student rhetorically crumpled up his paper after 10 minutes and growled, "You can't make me write this!") What does that imply about the rest of us? What would *you* do as a member of the opposite sex for a day? This last question is your essay assignment.

Exercise 2 Discussion and Critical Thinking

1. Why do you think the female students took to the assignment to write about "how each would spend a day as a member of his or her respective opposite sex"?

2. Why do you think the male students generally did not embrace the assignment?

3. What do the activities envisioned by the women and men imply about the ways they stereotype the opposite sex?

4. If you were an instructor giving the assignment, would you present the assignment differently? If so, how?

✳ Reading-Related Writing

"Men Are from Mars, Women Are from Venus"

1. Write an evaluation of the essay. How accurate are Gray's views? Does he oversimplify or stereotype? Might some people be offended by the gender images?
2. Apply Gray's gender characteristics to children in specific activities: their games, communications, dress, pastimes, hobbies, sports. (See Comparison and Contrast, page 24.)
3. Compare and contrast females and males or one specific representative from each gender. Consider concentrating on one

area—careers, driving style, dating, eating habits, or housekeeping—or consider three or more areas for points in your comparative study. (See Comparison and Contrast, page 24.)

"The Opposite Sex"

4. Write an essay in which you compare and contrast the reactions of the males and females. Include your interpretation of why the students presented the behavior of the opposite sexes as they did. (See Comparison and Contrast, page 24.)

Combined Reading Selections

5. Write an essay on the topic proposed by Doloff: Explain how you would spend a day in the guise of your opposite sex. Stay in gender character as you relate what you did (past tense) or are doing (present tense). Include relevant ideas from Gray's essay "Men Are from Mars, Women Are from Venus." Reflect on the content of Doloff's essay. (See Analysis by Division, page 18; Narration, page 15; and Exemplification, page 18.)

12

Fast Food Workers:
Robots or Thinkers?

What do thinking and workers in fast food establishments have in common? According to some, the answer is "nothing." According to others, the answer is "a lot." The jobs are held mainly by teenagers and immigrants. The pay is minimum. The respect is not worth mentioning. If you work(ed) in a fast food joint, would you flaunt that work experience or forget it on your job quest résumé? In other words, does it connect with "skill" or "stigma"? Do you wave your Mc-apron as a pennant of honor or cover your head with it?

These two essays express different views:

- "Behind the Counter" is concerned mainly with fast food chains, and the author says the model of corporate efficiency experts is the assembly line—the labor chain gang.
- "Low Wages, High Skills" offers a more positive view in a sociological study that broadens the definition of work to include how you get along with a coworker of a different look and language, and how you can fix the fry machine with a little kick or the cash register with a wad of gum.

Behind the Counter

Eric Schlosser

> *In his best-selling book* Fast Food Nation, *Eric Schlosser exposes an uninformed and largely uncaring society dependent on fast food. The industry itself is dependent on a system that consistently delivers the items quickly in an unvaryingly standard version. Schlosser explains just how that is accomplished.*

1   Every Saturday Elisa Zamot gets up at 5:15 in the morning. It's a struggle, and her head feels groggy as she steps into the shower. Her little sisters, Cookie and Sabrina, are fast asleep in their beds. By 5:30, Elisa's showered, done her hair, and put on her McDonald's uniform. She's sixteen, bright-eyed and olive-skinned, pretty and petite, ready for another day of work.

135

Elisa's mother usually drives her the half-mile or so to the restaurant, but sometimes Elisa walks, leaving home before the sun rises. Her family's modest townhouse sits beside a busy highway on the south side of Colorado Springs, in a largely poor and working-class neighborhood. Throughout the day, sounds of traffic fill the house, the steady whoosh of passing cars. But when Elisa heads for work, the streets are quiet, the sky's still dark, and the lights are out in the small houses and rental apartments along the road.

2   When Elisa arrives at McDonald's, the manager unlocks the door and lets her in. Sometimes the husband-and-wife cleaning crew are just finishing up. More often, it's just Elisa and the manager in the restaurant, surrounded by an empty parking lot. For the next hour or so, the two of them get everything ready. They turn on the ovens and grills. They go downstairs into the basement and get food and supplies for the morning shift. They get the paper cups, wrappers, cardboard containers, and packets of condiments. They step into the big freezer and get the frozen bacon, the frozen pancakes, and the frozen cinnamon rolls. They get the frozen hash browns, the frozen biscuits, the frozen McMuffins. They get the cartons of scrambled egg mix and orange juice mix. They bring the food upstairs and start preparing it before any customers appear, thawing some things in the microwave and cooking other things on the grill. They put the cooked food in special cabinets to keep it warm.

3   The restaurant opens for business at seven o'clock, and for the next hour or so, Elisa and the manager hold down the fort, handling all the orders. As the place starts to get busy, other employees arrive. Elisa works behind the counter. She takes orders and hands food to customers from breakfast through lunch. When she finally walks home, after seven hours of standing at a cash register, her feet hurt. She's wiped out. She comes through the front door, flops onto the living room couch, and turns on the TV. And the next morning she gets up at 5:15 again and starts the same routine.

4   Up and down Academy Boulevard, along South Nevada, Circle Drive, and Woodman Road, teenagers like Elisa run the fast food restaurants of Colorado Springs. Fast food kitchens often seem like a scene from *Bugsy Malone,* a film in which all the actors are children pretending to be adults. No other industry in the United States has a workforce so dominated by adolescents. About two-thirds of the nation's fast food workers are

under the age of twenty. Teenagers open the fast food outlets in the morning, close them at night, and keep them going at all hours in between. Even the managers and assistant managers are sometimes in their late teens. Unlike Olympic gymnastics—an activity in which teenagers consistently perform at a higher level than adults—there's nothing about the work in a fast food kitchen that requires young employees. Instead of relying upon a small, stable, well-paid, and well-trained workforce, the fast food industry seeks out part-time, unskilled workers who are willing to accept low pay. Teenagers have been the perfect candidates for these jobs, not only because they are less expensive to hire than adults, but also because their youthful inexperience makes them easier to control.

5   The labor practices of the fast food industry have their origins in the assembly line systems adopted by American manufacturers in the early twentieth century. Business historian Alfred D. Chandler has argued that a high rate of "throughput" was the most important aspect of these mass production systems. A factory's throughput is the speed and volume of its flow—a much more crucial measurement, according to Chandler, than the number of workers it employs or the value of its machinery. With innovative technology and the proper organization, a small number of workers can produce an enormous amount of goods cheaply. Throughput is all about increasing the speed of assembly, about doing things faster in order to make more.

6   Although the McDonald brothers had never encountered the term "throughput" or studied "scientific management," they instinctively grasped the underlying principles and applied them in the Speedee Service System. The restaurant operating scheme they developed has been widely adopted and refined over the past half century. The ethos of the assembly line remains at its core. The fast food industry's obsession with throughput has altered the way millions of Americans work, turned commercial kitchens into small factories, and changed familiar foods into commodities that are manufactured.

7   At Burger King restaurants, frozen hamburger patties are placed on a conveyor belt and emerge from a broiler ninety seconds later fully cooked. The ovens at Pizza Hut and at Domino's also use conveyor belts to ensure standardized cooking times. The ovens at McDonald's look like commercial laundry presses, with big steel hoods that swing down and grill hamburgers on both sides at once. The burgers, chicken, french fries, and buns

are all frozen when they arrive at a McDonald's. The shakes and sodas begin as syrup. At Taco Bell restaurants the food is "assembled," not prepared. The guacamole isn't made by workers in the kitchen; it's made at a factory in Michoacán, Mexico, then frozen and shipped north. The chain's taco meat arrives frozen and precooked in vacuum-sealed plastic bags. The beans are dehydrated and look like brownish corn flakes. The cooking process is fairly simple. "Everything's add water," a Taco Bell employee told me. "Just add hot water."

8   Although Richard and Mac McDonald introduced the division of labor to the restaurant business, it was a McDonald's executive named Fred Turner who created a production system of unusual thoroughness and attention to detail. In 1958, Turner put together an operations and training manual for the company that was seventy-five pages long, specifying how almost everything should be done. Hamburgers were always to be placed on the grill in six neat rows; french fries had to be exactly 0.28 inches thick. The McDonald's operations manual today has ten times the number of pages and weighs about four pounds. Known within the company as "the Bible," it contains precise instructions on how various appliances should be used, how each item on the menu should look, and how employees should greet customers. Operators who disobey these rules can lose their franchises. Cooking instructions are not only printed in the manual, they are often designed into the machines. A McDonald's kitchen is full of buzzers and flashing lights that tell employees what to do.

9   At the front counter, computerized cash registers issue their own commands. Once an order has been placed, buttons light up and suggest other menu items that can be added. Workers at the counter are told to increase the size of an order by recommending special promotions, pushing dessert, pointing out the financial logic behind the purchase of a larger drink. While doing so, they are instructed to be upbeat and friendly. "Smile with a greeting and make a positive first impression," a Burger King training manual suggests. "Show them you are GLAD TO SEE THEM. Include eye contact with the cheerful greeting."

10   The strict regimentation at fast food restaurants creates standardized products. It increases the throughput. And it gives fast food companies an enormous amount of power over their employees. "When management determines exactly how every task is to be done . . . and can impose its own rules about pace,

output, quality, and technique," the sociologist Robin Leidner has noted, "[it] makes workers increasingly interchangeable." The management no longer depends upon the talents or skills of its workers—those things are built into the operating system and machines. Jobs that have been "de-skilled" can be filled cheaply. The need to retain any individual worker is greatly reduced by the ease with which he or she can be replaced.

11   Teenagers have long provided the fast food industry with the bulk of its workforce. The industry's rapid growth coincided with the baby-boom expansion of that age group. Teenagers were in many ways the ideal candidates for these low-paying jobs. Since most teenagers still lived at home, they could afford to work for wages too low to support an adult, and until recently, their limited skills attracted few other employers. A job at a fast food restaurant became an American rite of passage, a first job soon left behind for better things. The flexible terms of employment in the fast food industry also attracted housewives who needed extra income. As the number of baby-boom teenagers declined, the fast food chains began to hire other marginalized workers: recent immigrants, the elderly, and the handicapped.

12   English is now the second language of at least one-sixth of the nation's restaurant workers, and about one-third of that group speaks no English at all. The proportion of fast food workers who cannot speak English is even higher. Many know only the names of the items on the menu; they speak "McDonald's English."

13   The fast food industry now employs some of the most disadvantaged members of American society. It often teaches basic job skills—such as getting to work on time—to people who can barely read, whose lives have been chaotic or shut off from the mainstream. Many individual franchisees are genuinely concerned about the well-being of their workers. But the stance of the fast food industry on issues involving employee training, the minimum wage, labor unions, and overtime pay strongly suggests that its motives in hiring the young, the poor, and the handicapped are hardly altruistic.

Exercise 1 Discussion and Critical Thinking

1. What are the main benefits of the assembly-line approach to producing and delivering the product?

2. What are the problems associated with using the assembly-line approach?

3. In reading this essay, what did you learn about fast food operation that you had not known?

4. Schlosser has observed and analyzed fast food production, but he has not worked in the fast food industry. If you have or if you know people who have worked in such establishments, what can you add to his account? Is his description accurate? Explain.

Low Wages, High Skills

Katherine S. Newman

> *As an anthropologist, Katherine S. Newman specializes in urban life and the working poor. This excerpt is from her well-researched, celebrated book* No Shame in My Game *(1999). As the title suggests, the workers have reasons for taking pride in what they do.*

1   Elise has worked the "drive-through" window at Burger Barn for the better part of three years. She is a virtuoso in a role that totally defeated one of my brightest doctoral students, who tried to work alongside her for a week or two. Her job pays only twenty-five cents above the minimum wage (after five years), but it requires that she listen to orders coming in through a speaker, send out a stream of instructions to co-workers who are preparing the food, pick up and check orders for customers already at the window, and receive money and make change, all more or less simultaneously. She has to make sure she keeps the sequence of orders straight so that the Big Burger goes to the man in the blue Mustang and not the woman right behind him in the red Camaro who has now revised her order for the third time. The memory and information-processing skills required to perform this job at a minimally acceptable level are considerable. Elise makes the operation look easy, but it clearly is a skilled job, as demanding as any of the dozen better-paid positions in the Post Office or the Gap stores where she has tried in vain to find higher-status employment.

2   This is not to suggest that working at Burger Barn is as complex as brain surgery. It is true that the component parts of the ballet, the multiple stations behind the counter, have been broken down into the simplest operations. Yet to make them work together under time pressure while minimizing wastage requires higher-order skills. We can think of these jobs as lowly, repetitive, routinized, and demeaning, or we can recognize that doing them right requires their incumbents to process information, coordinate with others, and track inventory. These valuable competencies are tucked away inside jobs that are popularly characterized as utterly lacking in skill.

3   If coordination were the only task required of these employees, then experience would probably eliminate the difficulty after a while. But there are many unpredictable events in the course of a workday that require some finesse to manage. Chief among them are abrasive encounters with customers, who [. . .] often have nothing better to do than rake a poor working stiff over the coals for a missing catsup packet or a batch of french fries that aren't quite hot enough. One afternoon at a Burger Barn cash register is enough to send most sane people into psychological counseling. It takes patience, forbearance, and an eye for the long-range goal (of holding on to your job, of impressing management with your fortitude) to get through some of these encounters. If ever there was an illustration of "people skills," this would be it.

4   Coping with rude customers and coordinating the many components of the production process are made all the more complex by the fact that in most Harlem Burger Barns, the workers hail from a multitude of countries and speak in a variety of languages. Monolingual Spanish speakers fresh from the Dominican Republic have to figure out orders spoken in Jamaican English. Puerto Ricans, who are generally bilingual, at least in the second generation, have to cope with the English dialects of African Americans. All of these people have to figure out how to serve customers who may be fresh off the boat from Guyana, West Africa, Honduras. The workplace melting pot bubbles along because people from these divergent groups are able to come together and learn bits and snatches of each other's languages—"workplace Spanish" or street English. They can communicate at a very rudimentary level in several dialects, and they know enough about each other's cultural traditions to be able to interpret actions, practices, dress styles, and

gender norms in ways that smooth over what can become major conflicts on the street.

5   In a world where residential segregation is sharp and racial antagonism no laughing matter, it is striking how well workers get along with one another. Friendships develop across lines that have hardened in the streets. Romances are born between African Americans and Puerto Ricans, legendary antagonists in the neighborhoods beyond the workplace. This is even more re-markable when one considers the competition that these groups are locked into in a declining labor market. They know very well that employers are using race- and class-based prefer-ences to decide who gets a job, and that their ability to foster the employment chances of friends and family members may well be compromised by a manager's racial biases. One can hear in their conversations behind the counter complaints about how they cannot get their friends jobs because—they believe— the manager wants to pick immigrants first and leave the native-born jobless. In this context, resentment builds against unfair barriers. Even so, workers of different ethnic back-grounds are able to reach across the walls of competition and cultural difference.

6   We are often admonished to remember that the United States is a multicultural society and that the workforce of the future will be increasingly composed of minorities and foreign-ers. Consultants make thousands of dollars advising companies in "diversity training" in order to manage the process of amal-gamation. Burger Barn is a living laboratory of diversity, the ul-timate melting pot for the working poor. They live in segre-gated spaces, but they work side by side with people whom they would rarely encounter on the block. If we regard the ability to work in a multiethnic, multilingual environment as a skill, as the consulting industry argues we should, then there is much to recommend the cultural capital acquired in the low-wage work-places of the inner city.

7   Restaurant owners are loath to cut their profits by calling in expensive repair services when their equipment breaks down, the plumbing goes out, or the electrical wiring blows. Indeed, general managers are required to spend time in training centers maintained by Burger Barn's corporate headquarters learning how to disassemble the machinery and rebuild it from scratch. The philosophers in the training centers say this is done to teach managers a "ground-up" appreciation for the equipment they are

working with. Any store owner will confess, however, that this knowledge is mainly good for holding labor costs down by making it unnecessary to call a repairman every time a milk shake machine malfunctions. What this means in practice is that managers much teach entry-level workers, especially the men (but the women as well), the art of mechanical repair and press them into service when the need strikes. Indeed, in one Harlem restaurant, workers had learned how to replace floor-to-ceiling windows (needed because of some bullet holes), a task they performed for well below the prevailing rates of a skilled glazier.

8   Then, of course, there is the matter of money. Burger Barn cash registers have been reengineered to make it possible for people with limited math abilities to operate them. Buttons on the face of the machine display the names of the items on the menu, and an internal program belts out the prices, adds them up, and figures out how much change is due a customer, all with no more than the push of a finger on the right "pad." Still, the workers who man the registers have to be careful to account for all the money that is in the till. Anything amiss and they are in deep trouble: they must replace any missing cash out of their wages. If money goes missing more than once, they are routinely fired. And money can disappear for a variety of reasons: someone makes a mistake in making change, an unexpected interloper uses the machine when the main register worker has gone into the back for some extra mustard packets, a customer changes her mind and wants to return an item (a transaction that isn't programmed into the machine). Even though much of the calculation involved in handling funds is done by computer chips, modest management skills are still required to keep everything in order.

9   While this is not computer programming, the demands of the job are nonetheless quite real. This becomes all too clear, even to managers who are of the opinion that these are "no-skill" jobs, when key people are missing. Workers who know the secrets of the trade—how to cut corners with the official procedures mandated by the company on food preparation, how to "trick" the cash register into giving the right amount of change when a mistake has been made, how to keep the orders straight when there are twenty people backed up in the drive-through line, how to teach new employees the real methods of food production (as opposed to the official script), and what to do when a customer throws a screaming fit and disrupts the

whole restaurant—keep the complicated ballet of fast food operation moving smoothly. When "experts" disappear from the
shift, nothing works the way it should. When they quit, the
whole crew is thrown into a state of near-chaos, a situation that
can take weeks to remedy as new people come "on line." If
these jobs were truly as denuded of skill as they are popularly
believed to be, none of this would matter. In fact, however, they
are richer in cognitive complexity and individual responsibility
than we acknowledge.

10   This is particularly evident when one watches closely over
time how new people are trained. Burger Barn, like most of its
competitors, has prepared training tapes designed to show new
workers with limited literacy skills how to operate the equipment, assemble the raw materials, and serve customers courte-
ously. Managers are told to use these tapes to instruct all new
crew members. In the real world, though, the tapes go missing,
the VCR machine doesn't work, and new workers come on
board in the middle of the hamburger rush hour when no one
has time to sit them down in front of a TV set for a lesson. They
have to be taught the old-fashioned way—person to person—
with the more experienced and capable workers serving as
teachers.

11   One of my graduate students learned this lesson the hard
way. A native of Puerto Rico, Ana Ramos-Zayas made her way
to a restaurant in the Dominican neighborhood of upper
Harlem and put on an apron in the middle of the peak midday
demand. Nobody could find the tapes, so she made do by trying
to mimic the workers around her. People were screaming at her
that she was doing it all wrong, but they were also moving like
greased lightning in the kitchen. Ana couldn't figure out how to
place the cheese on the hamburger patty so that it fit properly.
She tried it one way and then another—nothing came out right.
The experienced workers around her, who were all Spanish-
speakers, were not initially inclined to help her out, in part because they mistook her for a white girl—something they had
not seen behind the counter before. But when they discovered,
quite by accident, that Ana was a Latina (she muttered a Spanish curse upon dropping the fifth bun in a row), they embraced
her as a fellow migrant and quickly set about making sure she
understood the right way to position the cheese.

12   From that day forward, these workers taught Ana all there
was to know about the french fry machine, about how to get a

milk shake to come out right, about the difference between cooking a fish sandwich and a chicken sandwich, and about how to forecast demand for each so that the bins do not overfill and force wastage. Without their help, provided entirely along informal lines, Ana would have been at sea. Her experience is typical in the way it reveals the hidden knowledge locked up inside what appears to surface observers (and to many employees themselves) as a job that requires no thinking, no planning, and no skill.

13 As entry-level employment, fast food jobs provide the worker with experience and knowledge that ought to be useful as a platform for advancement in the work world. After all, many white-collar positions require similar talents: memory skills, inventory management, the ability to work with a diverse crowd of employees, and versatility in covering for fellow workers when the demand increases. Most jobs require "soft skills" in people management, and those that involve customer contact almost always require the ability to placate angry clients. With experience of this kind, Burger Barn workers ought to be able to parlay their "human capital" into jobs that will boost their incomes and advance them up the status ladder.

14 The fact that this happens so rarely is only partially a function of the diplomas they lack or the mediocre test scores they have to offer employers who use these screening devices. They are equally limited by the popular impression that the jobs they hold now are devoid of value. The fast food industry's reputation for deskilling its work combines with the low social standing of these inner-city employees to make their skills invisible. Employers with better jobs to offer do recognize that Burger Barn veterans are disciplined: they show up for work on time, they know how to serve the public. Yet if the jobs they are trying to fill require more advanced skills (inventory, the ability to learn new technologies, communication skills), Burger Barn is just about the last place that comes to mind as an appropriate proving ground. A week behind the counter of the average fast food restaurant might convince them otherwise, but employers are not anthropologists out looking for a fresh view of entry-level employment. They operate on the basis of assumptions that are widely shared and have neither the time nor the inclination to seek out the hidden skills that Burger Barn employees have developed.

15 Perhaps fast food veterans would do better in the search for good jobs if they could reveal that hidden reservoir of

human capital. But they are as much the victims of the poor reputation of their jobs as the employers they now seek to impress. When we asked them to explain the skills involved in their work, they invariably looked at us in surprise: "Any fool could do this job. Are you kidding?" They saw themselves as sitting at the bottom of the job chain and the negative valence of their jobs as more or less justified. A lot of energy goes into living with that "truth" and retaining some sense of dignity, but that effort does not involve rethinking the reputation of their work as skillfree. Hence they are the last people to try to overturn a stereotype and sell themselves to other employers as workers who qualify for better jobs.

16   I have suggested here that neither the employers nor the job-seekers have got it right. There are competencies involved in these jobs that should be more widely known and more easily built upon as the basis for advancement in the labor market. Yet even if we could work some magic along these lines, the limitations built into the social networks of most low-wage workers in the inner city could make it hard to parlay that new reputation into success.

Exercise 2 Discussion and Critical Thinking

1. Newman maintains that low-wage workers in this ordinary fast food establishment perform tasks that require exceptional skills. To reach her conclusion, she uses analysis by division. Fill in the blanks to indicate how she proceeded.

   Unit (What is she concerned with?):

   Principle of function (What aspect does she focus on?):

   Parts based on the principle (What are those potentially transferable skills?)

   ■

   ■

   ■

   ■

■

■

2. Could the transferable skills discussed in this essay be included effectively on a résumé for a person seeking a higher-paying job?

3. Have you held a low-paying job that required important transferable skills? Discuss.

4. Do you agree with the author's conclusions? Why or why not?

5. How do you interpret the last sentence in the essay: "Yet even if we could work some magic along these lines, the limitations built into the social networks of most low-wage workers in the inner city could make it hard to parlay that new reputation into success"?

✳ Reading-Related Writing

"Behind the Counter"

1. Using Schlosser's essay as a model, write about a job you have had that used an assembly-line approach to production or service. (See Exemplification, page 18.)
2. If you have had experience working in a fast food establishment or if you know someone who has, evaluate Schlosser's essay, pointing out to what extent it is or is not correct.
3. If you have worked in an establishment that did not use the methods described by Schlosser, compare and contrast the methods described by Schlosser with the ones you are familiar with. (See Comparison and Contrast, page 24.)

"Low Wages, High Skills"

4. Write a summary of this essay, stressing the transferable skills Newman uses to judge the nature of the work at Burger Barn. Consider making your writing a two-part response (see page 7).

5. Write an essay about a low-wage job you once held. Explain how you learned and practiced transferable skills that helped you in other jobs or other life situations. The skills will be the parts of your analysis by division. Some of these skills may be the same as, or similar to, the ones discussed by Newman. Using references to her essay may enrich your own.

Combined Reading Selections

6. Newman stresses the overlooked transferable skills in the fast food establishment she studied; Schlosser sees no significant transferable skills in the fast food chain operations. Compare and contrast the two views. Do the authors disagree or are they talking about different kinds of establishments? (See Comparison and Contrast, page 24.)

13

Bullies 'R' Us?

Few people go through school without being bullied by someone. The victims may at times be bullies themselves. Bullies come in different shapes, colors, and genders. Their destructive work takes different forms and has different effects, ranging through psychological and physical. The larger group seems to seek out those who are different—largeness, smallness, conspicuously distinguishing features, name, race, sexual preference, behavior. In a recent study, a girl said she was picked on for ten years of schooling for bad teeth and then it stopped. She was asked why it stopped. She was embarrassed but finally said she had found someone worse off than she was and started making fun of her. Others joined her in the ridicule, and she was free. And so it goes.

The reading selections in this chapter include one discussion of definitions and three examples of students who just happened to be different.

- "Bully, Bully" says definitions sometimes are too broad.
- "No Tears for Frankie" tells of the death of a childhood nemesis.
- "Walk in My Full-Figure Shoes" says, "*Fat* is only a word, not a human being."
- "Someone Is Listening" explains what being a gay child is like, inside the closet and out.

Bully, Bully

John Leo

> *John Leo, staff writer for* U.S. News and World Report, *offers his observations on the currently hot-button issue of bullying in the United States. Focusing on definitions in a national study, he argues that rumors and dirty looks and putting up with horrible classmates are all part of growing up and should not be classified as bullying.*

Do Gossip and Rumors Count as Punishable Behavior?

1   Now we have a big national study on bullying, and the problem with it is right there in the first paragraph: Bullying behavior may be "verbal (e.g., name-calling, threats), physical (e.g., hitting), or psychological (e.g., rumors, shunning/exclusion)." Uh-oh. The study may or may not have put bullying on the map as a major national issue. But it rather clearly used a dubious tactic: taking a lot of harmless and minor things ordinary children do and turning them into examples of bullying. Calling somebody a jerk and spreading rumors counted as bullying in the study. Repeated teasing counted too. You achieved bully status if you didn't let the class creep into your game of catch, or if you just stayed away from people you didn't like (shunning, exclusion).

2   With a definition like that, the total of children involved in either bullying or being bullied themselves ought to be around 100 percent. But no, the bullying study says only 29.9 percent of the students studied reported frequent or moderate involvement—and that total was arrived at by lumping bullies and their victims together in the statistics.

Debatable Definitions

3   The low numbers and highly debatable definitions undercut the study's conclusion that bullying is "a serious problem for U.S. youth." Of the 29.9 figure, 13.0 percent were bullies, 10.6 percent were targets of bullying, and 6.3 percent were both perpetrators and victims. The study, done by the National Institute of Child Health and Human Development, is based on 15,686 questionnaires filled out by students in grades six through 10 in public and private schools around the country.

4   We have seen this statistical blending of serious and trivial incidents before. The American Association of University Women produced a 1993 report showing that 80 percent of American students have been sexually harassed, including a hard-to-believe 76 percent of all boys. The AAUW got the numbers up that high by including glances, gestures, gossip, and naughty jokes. The elastic definition encouraged schools and courts to view many previously uncontroversial kinds of expression as sexual harassment. Before long, schools were making solemn lists of harassing behaviors that included winking, and calling someone "honey."

5   Another set of broad definitions appeared when zero-tolerance policies descended on the schools. Antidrug rules were extended to cover aspirin. Antiweapons regulations covered a rubber knife used in a school play. Just two months ago, a third grader in Monroe, La., was suspended for drawing a picture of G.I. Joe. Now the antibullying movement is poised to provide a third source of dubious hyperregulation of the young. One antibullying specialist says "hard looks" and "stare downs"—everyday activities for millions of hormone-driven adolescents—should be punishable offenses under student codes.

6   This has all the makings of an antibullying crusade with many of the same wretched excesses of the zero-tolerance and antiharassment campaigns. Serious bullying can be ugly. Parents and schools should stop it and punish offenders. And schools should do whatever they can to create a culture of civility and tolerance. But rumors and dirty looks and putting up with horrible classmates are a part of growing up. So are the teenage tendencies to form cliques and snub people now and then. Adults shouldn't faint when they see this behavior, or try to turn it into quasi-criminal activity.

7   Another pitfall: in focusing on gossip, rumors, and verbal offenses, the crusade has the obvious potential to infringe on free speech at schools. Will comments like "I think Catholicism is wrong," or "I think homosexuality is a sin," be turned into antibullying offenses? The crusade could also demonize those who bully, instead of helping them change. Some of the antibully literature circulating in Europe is hateful stuff. One screed calls "the serial bully" glib, shallow, evasive, incapable of intimacy, and a practiced liar who "displays a seemingly limitless demonic energy." Yet a lot of the academic literature reports that bullies often aren't very psychologically different from their victims. And the national study says a fifth of bullying victims are bullies themselves.

8   The example of Europe's more advanced antibullying crusade should make Americans cautious. The European campaign has expanded from schools into the adult world and the workplace. Several nations are considering antibullying laws, including Britain. Definitions are expanding too. A proposed antibullying law in Portugal would make it illegal to harass workers by giving them tasks for which they are overqualified. Deliberately giving employees erroneous information would count as bullying too. Ireland's antibullying task force came up with a scarily vague

definition of bullying: "repeated inappropriate behavior, direct or indirect," which could "reasonably be regarded as undermining the individual's right to dignity at work." Imagine what the American litigation industry could do with wording like that.

9   It's time to stop and ask: Where is our antibullying campaign going?

Exercise 1   Discussion and Critical Thinking

1. Underline the thesis sentence.

2. The definition in question defines *bullying* as "verbal, physical, or psychological" behavior directed against the victim. Of those three characteristics, which two does Leo find troublesome?

3. Why does Leo find those two characteristics troublesome?

4. Does he have a good point in criticizing the definition or is he unfairly ridiculing the definition?

5. Does Leo believe there should be no antibullying campaign?

No Tears for Frankie

Gina Greenlee

> *In this essay, freelance writer Gina Greenlee recalls a childhood peer. He died. She attended his funeral. She rejoiced. This article was first published in the "Lives" section of the* New York Times Magazine.

1   I was in the fifth grade when Frankie died. It was 1971. My whole class planned to attend the funeral, since we knew him. My father thought going might give me nightmares, but I insisted. I had never seen a dead person before. Most of all, I wanted to be sure that the little creep would never touch me again.

2   Frankie lived in Lower Manhattan where run-down tenements along Avenues A, B and C were on the verge of becoming

the crack houses of the '80s. At the time, I lived nearby. Then in 1970 my family moved into an apartment in Coop Village on Grand Street and F.D.R. Drive. It was only three blocks—and a world—away from the projects to a predominantly white middle-class community on the East River. Overnight at school, I became "that black girl who lives in the rich Jew buildings." Or at least that's what Frankie and my other African-American classmates thought I was. It became a familiar chant of theirs as I made my way through my old neighborhood to get to school.

3   Frankie and I were in the same grade, but I was 10 and he was 12 because he had been left back twice. He tormented all of the girls in our class. But Frankie relished singling me out— the only black girl in a sea of Jewish girls dotted with Latinas— and he had done so since I first arrived from another school in third grade.

4   He never did any schoolwork. Instead, for the first three periods Frankie's curriculum was mayhem; by fourth period he was usually in the principal's office; and by the fifth, he was back in class unremorseful and pumped to do it again. He only got worse in that working-class, urban-blight panacea, the after-school program. It was a nice idea: children whose parents were unavailable at 3 o'clock because they were working stayed after school to study, improve skills and tackle extra-credit projects. I spent those afternoons trying to stay alive.

5   Frankie and his crew would grab my breasts, genitals and buttocks when the teachers weren't looking. Their hands, quick as filthy street rats, darted across my private parts in assembly line, during dance rehearsals and yard processions. They would leave scrawled notes in my book bag that read, "I'm gonna beat you up after school," or "I'll get you in the stairwell."

6   One spring afternoon, I had made it through another harrowing two hours after school, only to be cornered on the stairs by the whole nasty lot. They taunted me to walk down ahead of them. I managed each step as if it were my first, balancing myself on the chalk-blue shellacked handrail as I peered through the landing divider reminiscent of a wire cage, hoping to see another student, teacher, anyone. Frankie shoved me, and I tumbled one full flight, landing on my knees, my favorite brown plaid dress above my ears, easy pickings for the tiny vultures who cackled obscenities while snatching at my body, punching and kicking me. That day, I understood the depth of Frankie's perversity.

7   When I told a friend that our classroom emptied out at 3 P.M., leaving me alone with Frankie's boys, without having to share another detail, she said, "Come to my house after school." I had enjoyed two afternoons of baking cookies and doll playing when I let slip that my parents thought I was in class. My friend's mother welcomed me to play at her home anytime as long as my parents knew. "Why were you at Amy's and not in the after-school program?" my father asked me later that night. I didn't tell him because I didn't think he could help me. His interventions would only inspire retaliations and spiral me deeper into the mess.

8   I did try to tell my teachers, but nobody believed me. They chuckled and said, "Frankie just has a crush on you." That's what I told my father 15 years after the attacks, when he asked me if I had told my teachers. I guess in their world, 12-year-old boys don't sexually attack 10-year-old girls. What world did they come from, anyway? What world was I in, and how could I fix it so Frankie would disappear?

9   One morning when my teachers had stepped away from the classroom, Frankie and his boys shoved me into the coat closet and held the door shut while I was alone with Frankie. It was dark. As he kept touching me, I tried to push him away and screamed to be let out. But Frankie's friends held steadfast until the teachers arrived; then they scrambled to their seats. None of the other kids said a word. But in front of them all, I told Frankie that I hated his guts and hoped he would die.

10   Quite accommodating, he lay in a casket later that year. I didn't shed a tear. My heart was hardened, though. As usual, Frankie was up to no good—tampering with public property with the boys—when he got himself electrocuted. I was 10, and I was glad.

Exercise 2   Discussion and Critical Thinking

1. Use phrases or sentences to indicate these parts of this narrative:

Situation:

Conflict:

Struggle:

Outcome:

Meaning:

2. Why didn't Greenlee shed a tear?

3. Having read this essay, do you think that this event made Greenlee generally a more compassionate or a less compassionate human being? Explain.

4. Is this an essay that only a person who has been bullied dreadfully can understand or can it be appreciated by anyone? Explain.

5. What would you say to people who would have forgiven Frankie in his casket?

Walk in My Full-Figure Shoes

Karen Peterson

Even in this era of political correctness, a few social transgressions are allowed to go unchecked. Student Karen Peterson would like to persuade her audience to examine one of these free fire zones. If you meet her, you will see a woman who is hardworking, highly competent, and witty. She says she has experienced all of the negative things you are going to read about, but she accepts herself for what she is—a proud and beautiful woman with a lot of confidence, intelligence, sensitivity, and self-fulfillment, who just happens to be overweight.

1 Let's play the *if* game. . . . If you have never experienced being called bubbles, two-ton Tessie, chunky, or plump; if you have never walked into a store and been told, "We don't carry your size"; if you have never experienced being left out of a trip to the beach by a group of your peers; if you have never been the last one chosen for a team and then sent to right field; if you have never been rejected by a friend who was becoming popular with the "in" crowd; if you have never been laughed at when

you sat in a tiny chair; if you have never dreamed of being a cheerleader or a homecoming queen, then you have never been fat. But if you have, you know that society as a whole views being fat as unacceptable, and this stereotype has devastating psychological effects. Society seems to believe that fat people are unhealthy, unhappy, low in self-esteem, unmotivated, and lazy, to name just a few of the unwarranted labels.

2   I am overweight, but I do not fit the stereotype. I am in great health. I am subject to the same emotions as those of a thin person. As far as having low self-esteem, I like myself and am secure in who I am. With regard to being unmotivated and lazy, I go to school full-time (17 semester units), and I take care of a household of four. I make the White Tornado look sluggish by comparison.

3   The fashion industry, which is also dictated to by society, has long ignored the "full figure." When I was growing up, it was difficult to find fashionable, stylish clothing that fit me. Most clothing manufacturers designed clothes for the tall and thin figure, even though the world's population has few of those shapes. I often found myself going from store to store, discovering that the only place that carried my size was called something like Coleman Tents R Us. This may seem funny, but for a person like me, it can be traumatic.

4   The media contribute to stereotyping by promoting the idea that in order to be beautiful, happy, healthy, and loved, a person must be thin. They promote this concept by showing thin people exclusively when they advertise cosmetics, clothing, cars, and alcohol. Only thin people are seen enjoying themselves on vacations. It's no wonder that fat people feel overwhelmed and defeated, when this is the image they continually see on virtually every television commercial, billboard, and magazine cover. These concepts and images create extreme pressure to conform. For instance, Oprah Winfrey was subjected to pressure and ridicule when one diet didn't work. She failed to fit the media's image. But she was still the same person. Surely a person is worth more than an image, heavy or light. Like her, I'm worth more than a perfect image.

5   The worst offender of social stereotyping of fat people is the health-and-fitness industry. No other industry can do more psychological and physical damage while making a bundle of money by exploiting fat people. With all the fad diets, quick-weight-loss pills, "miracle" fat creams, and exercise weight-loss videos, it is no wonder that fat people don't know whom to believe, which

weight-loss guru to follow, or simply how to lose weight success-
fully and safely. All of the marketed diets and solutions seem to
place great emphasis on being fit and healthy. Yet in reality,
many are detrimental. For most of my life, I have tried a variety
of these so-called get-thin-quick regimens. The outcome at first
was always great, but they fail to help me maintain the new, thin
look. What resulted is commonly known as the yo-yo syndrome.
I lost weight, but once I stopped dieting, the old habit and pounds
returned, sometimes accompanied by even *more* pounds.

6   But as pounds come and pounds go, people really need to
look past the scales and accept others for what they are. I invite
all to come walk in my full-figure shoes as we continue the *if*
game. . . . If you have never cried yourself to sleep and wished
for a fairy godmother to transform your body; if you have never
been treated as if you were invisible and wished you really
were; if you have never been made to feel unlovable by those
who are unworthy of your love; if you have never forced yourself to laugh at a joke about weight and wanted the teller punished; if you have never known the pain of those things, then
you have never been fat. *Fat* is only a word, not a human being.
Fat cannot feel, need, or want as I have and as I still do.

Exercise 3   Discussion and Critical Thinking

1. Why is this essay one of persuasion but not argument?

2. Why is an essay of only persuasion, such as this one, less likely
   to have a refutation than an essay of argument?

3. According to Peterson, does more discrimination occur during
   youth or adulthood?

4. How does Peterson make her support more specific?

5. What techniques does she use in writing her introduction and
   conclusion?

Someone Is Listening

Michael Holguin

Student Michael Holguin grew up with shame and guilt because he believed he was wicked. His belief was implanted and reinforced by all institutions he encountered—family, church, school, and government. It was wrong in every sense to be sexually attracted to people of the same gender. Therefore, he knew he must keep his mortal sin a secret.

1   In today's society there is a form of child abuse that not even Oprah talks about. Unlike some other forms of abuse, it knows no limitations—no ethnic, no religious, no educational, and no socioeconomic boundaries. Lives are destroyed by parents who act in fear and ignorance. Dreams are shattered by the cruel and hurtful words of friends. Every day, hundreds of gay youths hide in their rooms and cry from pain caused by the mean and careless behavior of those who claim to love them.

2   In a Judeo-Christian society it is common for families to attend church with their children. The pastor in many of these churches stands at the podium and announces, "Homosexuals are an abomination unto the Lord." The church walls shake from the resounding "Amen" from the congregation. The pastor continues, "Homosexuals are sick. Perverted. They are a danger to our children." In agreement the congregation once more says, "Amen." I know how this feels. As a gay person, I recall the pain of many Sundays during my childhood. I prayed extra hard for God's cure before someone would find out my secret and embarrass me and my family, because I remembered what had happened to a friend the year before. So I kept answering the altar call every Sunday when the unwanted feeling wouldn't go away. The fear of rejection and eternal damnation made me too terrified to confide in anyone or to ask for help. After all, my parents seemed to tell me I deserved such a fate every time they said, "Amen."

3   Every day at school became more difficult to endure. I faced the jokes in the locker room. Even my best friend told some, and occasionally, to keep from being discovered, I told some. At this point, how much self-esteem could I have had? I cringed when my coach urged us to "kick those faggots' asses" but I still kicked. Yet every day my feelings were denied. My health teacher told us, "Someday you will all grow up and get married and have

children." I couldn't understand why I had no such desire. I would turn on the television, and there would be a cop show on. This week's criminal was a gay child molester . . . again. I think "Baretta" had the same story the week before. I changed the station to "Barney Miller," where there was an old man wearing a polyester jumpsuit and a silk scarf around his neck, and talking with a lisp. Couldn't they drop the lisp just once, I wonder. I cringe, thinking this is my inevitable fate, my curse.

4   By the time I reached my teen years, I'd heard and seen so much negativity toward my "condition" that my life at home became plagued with constant fears. I became afraid of rejection. I knew my Christian family would think I was sick, perverted, and dangerous to children. Dad would be disappointed, even though I had six brothers to carry on the family name. Mom would not want me around because she'd worry about what to tell Grandma and Grandpa. My brother would pretend he didn't know me at school.

5   My fears were reinforced by close-up examples. Once I had a friend named Daniel, who was the son of a local preacher. I don't know where Daniel got the nerve at the age of twelve to tell his parents he was gay, but that's what he did. It was also at the age of twelve that his father put him out on the street after all the beatings failed to cure him. Daniel managed to stay alive on the streets as a prostitute. He's in prison now, dying of AIDS. The fear of rejection was real.

6   I learned how to fit in out of fear of humiliation but especially out of fear of physical abuse. I had seen Daniel's father and brothers beat him up almost daily. An even earlier memory from when I was very young involved a boy named Terry, who everyone knew was different. Some kids had figured Terry out. One day behind the school, way out in the field, four kids beat Terry up. Kicking and slugging him as he fell to the ground, they called out "Sissy" and "Queer" as they swung at him. We had only heard the word *queer* from the older boys, and no one was sure what it meant exactly. We hadn't encountered the word *faggot* yet. I suppose I didn't like Terry much either, but I felt bad as I watched in terror, knowing that the next time it could be me that they considered "different."

7   After years of living with low self-esteem, a battered self-image, and a secret life, one's psyche tends to give out. The highest rate of teen suicide is among gay youths. In a recent five-year study, it was determined that fear of rejection

was the number one cause of suicide among gay teenagers. After losing the loving environment of friends and families, many gays turn to other means for comfort. Drug and alcohol abuse is high among gays. Many turn to multiple lovers, looking for acceptance and emotional support. The result of this has been the devastating spread of AIDS. With nowhere to go, suicide often seems to be the only option. My friend Billy, when visiting his younger sister at his mother's home, would have to stay on the front porch and talk through the screen door at his mother's request. Last February, at the age of 18, Billy drove up to the mountains and there took his own life. Before he died he wrote on the hood of his car, "God, help me." I recall my own suicide attempt, which was the result of my inability to deal with a life-style everyone close to me was unable to accept. It was only my self-acceptance that eventually saved me from being a statistic.

8   When planning a family, people should ask themselves, "Will I love my children for who they are, or will I love them only if they're what I want them to be?" If people answer the latter, they shouldn't be parents. The same kind of thing might be said for others who are responsible for helping children develop. Abuse comes in many forms, and ignorance and self-centeredness are usually its foundation. Parents, preachers, teachers, clergy, friends—please be cautious of what you say. The children are listening.

Exercise 4   Discussion and Critical Thinking

1. What are the sources of abuse of gay youth?

2. Why does this kind of abuse go largely unreported?

3. What is Holguin's main support? Underline and annotate the assertion (proposition) and the supporting points.

4. How did Holguin survive?

✳ Reading-Related Writing

"Bully, Bully"

1. Evaluate Leo's essay, either agreeing or disagreeing with his view that the definition of bullying is often too broad. (See Definition, page 26; Argument, page 28; and Cause and Effect, page 21.)
2. Using Leo's essay as a model, write your own definition of bullying. Like Leo, explain what is and what is not bullying. Include examples from your observations about bullying. (See Definition, page 26, and Exemplification, page 18.)

"No Tears for Frankie"

3. Write a two-part response in which you summarize what occurred and comment on Greenlee's behavior and feelings. Under the circumstances, would you have expected her to feel any sympathy or compassion for her deceased tormentor? (See two-part response, page 7.)
4. Using this essay as a model, write about a time when you were a victim of a bully. How did you feel at the time? How did you feel later, especially if you had the occasion to see the bully again? (See Narration, page 15.)

"Walk in My Full-Figure Shoes"

5. Write an essay of persuasion in which you discuss the causes and effects of discrimination against a group of people with a common characteristic. Possible topics include the causes and effects of discrimination in relation to name, race, religion, body adornment, sexual preference, weight, height, baldness, or physical handicap. (See Argument, page 28.)

"Someone Is Listening"

6. Write an essay in which you advocate some specific kind of education that would alleviate the problem of discrimination against gays in schools. (See Argument, page 28.)
7. Pretend that you are a sympathetic parent of a gay child and explain how you would help your child to cope with attitudes in society.

8. Discuss this problem from a lesbian perspective. Is it essentially the same or different? Explain. (See Comparison and Contrast, page 24.)

9. Write about why some people have such strong negative reactions to homosexuality. (See Cause and Effect, page 21.)

10. Write an argument in which you are the advocate for another type of "outsider" such as a minority in terms of race, religion, political or philosophical beliefs, or medical condition. (See Argument, page 28.)

Combined Reading Selections

11. Write an essay in which you apply Leo's definition to one or more of the other three essays. (See Definition, page 26, and Analysis by Division, page 18.)

12. In paragraph 7 of "Bully, Bully," Leo poses this question: "Will comments like 'I think Catholicism is wrong' or 'I think homosexuality is a sin' be turned into antibullying offenses?" He sees potential infringement on free speech and a possible demonization of those charged with bullying. How does his concern relate to the views of Peterson in "Walk in My Full-Figure Shoes" and Holguin in "Someone Is Listening"? Explain how they might react to what he says throughout his essay.

✳ Appendix

Handbook

This handbook presents rules and examples for grammar, usage, punctuation, and capitalization. One good way to practice basic writing skills is to write your own examples. In working with verb tense, for example, you could write sentences (perhaps similar to the model sentences) in which you apply the appropriate patterns. In working with punctuation, you could write sentences that demonstrate your ability to use different punctuation marks correctly.

✳ Subjects and Verbs

The **subject** is what the sentence is about, and the **verb** indicates what the subject is doing or is being.

Subjects

You can recognize the **simple subject** by asking *Who?* or *What?* causes the action or expresses the state of being found in the verb.

1. The simple subject and the simple verb can be single or compound.

   My *friend* and *I* have much in common.

   My friend *came* and *left* a present.

2. Although the subject usually appears before the verb, it may follow the verb.

   From tiny acorns grow mighty *oaks.*

3. The **command,** or **imperative,** sentence has a "you" as the implied subject, and no stated subject.

   (*You*) Read the notes.

4. Be careful not to confuse a subject with an object of a preposition.

> The *foreman* [subject] of the *jury* [object of the preposition] directs discussion.

Verbs

Verbs show action or express being in relation to the subject.

1. **Action verbs** show movement or accomplishment of an idea or a deed.

> He *dropped* the book. (movement)
> He *read* the book. (accomplishment)

2. *Being* **verbs** indicate existence.

> They *were* concerned.

3. Verbs may appear as single words or as phrases.

> He *led* the charge. (single word)
> She *is leading* the charge. (phrase)

4. Verbs that are joined by a coordinating conjunction such as *and* and *or* are called **compound verbs.**

> She *worked* for twenty-five years and *retired.*

5. Do not confuse verbs with **verbals,** verblike words that function as other parts of speech.

> The bird *singing* [participle acting as an adjective] in the tree is defending its territory.
> *Singing* [gerund acting as a noun subject] is fun.
> I want *to eat* [infinitive acting as a noun object].

6. Do not confuse **adverbs** such as *never, not,* and *hardly* with verbs; they only modify verbs.
7. Do not overlook a part of the verb that is separated from another in a question.

> Where *had* the defendant *gone* on that fateful night?

✳ Kinds of Sentences

On the basis of number and kinds of clauses, sentences may be classified as simple, compound, complex, and compound-complex.

Clauses

1. A **clause** is a group of words with a subject and a verb that functions as a part or all of a complete sentence. There are two kinds of clauses: independent (main) and dependent (subordinate).

2. An **independent (main) clause** is a group of words with a subject and a verb that can stand alone and make sense. An independent clause expresses a complete thought by itself and can be written as a separate sentence.

    I have the money.

3. A **dependent clause** is a group of words with a subject and a verb that depends on a main clause to give it meaning. The dependent clause functions in the common sentence patterns as a noun, an adjective, or an adverb.

    When I have the money

Kinds of Sentences Defined

Kind	Definition	Example
1. Simple	One independent clause	She did the work well.
2. Compound	Two or more independent clauses	She did the work well, and she was paid well.
3. Complex	One independent clause and one or more dependent clauses	*Because she did the work well,* she was paid well.
4. Compound-Complex	Two or more independent clauses and one or more dependent clauses	*Because she did the work well,* she was paid well, and she was satisfied.

Punctuation

1. Use a comma before a coordinating conjunction (*for, and, nor, but, or, yet, so*) between two independent clauses.

    The movie was good, *but* the tickets were expensive.

2. Use a comma after a dependent clause (beginning with a subordinating conjunction such as *because, although, when, since,* or *before*) that occurs before the main clause.

    When the bus arrived, we quickly boarded.

3. Use a semicolon between two independent clauses in one sentence if there is no coordinating conjunction.

> The bus arrived; we quickly boarded.

4. Use a semicolon before and usually a comma after a conjunctive adverb (such as *however, otherwise, therefore, on the other hand,* and *in fact*), and between two independent clauses (no comma after *then, also, now, thus,* and *soon*).

> The Dodgers have not played well this year; *however,* the Giants have won ten games in a row.

> Spring training went well; then the regular baseball season began.

✳ Sentence Problems

Fragments

A correct sentence signals completeness; a **fragment** (a group of words without a subject, without a verb, or without both) signals incompleteness—it doesn't make sense. You would expect the speaker or writer of a fragment to say or write more or to rephrase it.

1. A **dependent clause,** which begins with a subordinating word, cannot stand by itself.

> *Because* he left.
>
> *When* she worked.
>
> *Although* they slept.

2. A **verbal phrase,** a **prepositional phrase,** and an **appositive phrase** may carry ideas, but each is incomplete because it lacks a subject and a verb.

> VERBAL PHRASE   *having studied hard all evening*
> SENTENCE   Having studied hard all evening, John decided to retire.
>
> PREPOSITIONAL PHRASE   *in the store*
> SENTENCE   She worked in the store.
>
> APPOSITIVE PHRASE   *a successful business*
> SENTENCE   Marks Brothers, a successful business, sells clothing.

3. Each complete sentence must have an **independent clause,** meaning a word or a group of words that contains a subject and a verb that can stand alone.

> *He enrolled* for the fall semester.

Comma Splices and Run-Ons

The **comma splice** consists of two independent clauses with only a comma between them.

The weather was disappointing, <u>we canceled the picnic.</u>

A comma by itself cannot join two independent clauses.

The **run-on** differs from the comma splice in only one respect: it has no comma between the independent clauses. Therefore, the run-on is two independent clauses with *nothing* between them.

The weather was disappointing <u>we canceled the picnic.</u>

Independent clauses must be properly connected.

Correct comma splices and run-ons by using a coordinating conjunction, a subordinating conjunction, or a semicolon, or by making each clause a separate sentence.

1. Use a comma and a **coordinating conjunction** (*for, and, nor, but, or, yet, so*).

   We canceled the picnic, *for* the weather was disappointing.

2. Use a **subordinating conjunction** (such as *because, after, that, when, although, since, how, until, unless, before*) to make one clause dependent.

   Because the weather was disappointing, we canceled the picnic.

3. Use a **semicolon** (with or without a conjunctive adverb such as *however, otherwise, therefore, similarly, hence, on the other hand, then, consequently, also, thus*).

   The weather was disappointing; we canceled the picnic.
   The weather was disappointing; *therefore,* we canceled the picnic.

4. Make each clause a separate sentence. For a comma splice, replace the comma with a period, and begin the second sentence (clause) with a capital letter. For a run-on, insert a period between the two independent clauses and begin the second sentence with a capital letter.

   The weather was disappointing. We canceled the picnic.

❋ Sentence Combining

Coordination

If you intend to communicate two equally important and closely related ideas, you certainly will want to place them close together, probably in a **compound sentence** (two or more independent clauses).

1. When you combine two sentences by using a coordinating conjunction, drop the period, change the capital letter to a small letter, and insert a comma before the coordinating conjunction.

    He likes your home. He can visit for only three months.

    He likes your home, *but* he can visit for only three months.

2. When you combine two sentences by using a semicolon, replace the period with a semicolon and change the capital letter to a small letter. If you wish to use a conjunctive adverb, insert it after the semicolon and usually put a comma after it.

    He likes your home; he can visit for only three months.

    He likes your home; *however,* he can visit for only three months.

Subordination

If you have two ideas that are closely related, but one is secondary or dependent on the other, you may want to use a complex sentence.

    My neighbors are considerate. They never play loud music.

    Because my neighbors are considerate, they never play loud music.

1. If the dependent clause comes before the main clause, set it off with a comma.

    Before you dive, be sure there is water in the pool.

2. If the dependent clause comes *after* or *within* the main clause, set it off with a comma only if you use the word *though* or *although,* or if the words are not necessary to convey the basic meaning in the sentence.

    Be sure there is water in the pool *before you dive.*

Coordination and Subordination

At times you may want to show the relationship of three or more ideas within one sentence. If that relationship involves two or more main ideas and one or more supporting ideas, the combination can be stated in a **compound-complex sentence** (two or more independent clauses and one or more dependent clauses).

Before he learned how to operate a computer, he had trouble
        dependent clause   independent clause
with his typewritten assignments, but now he produces clean,
                                                        independent clause
attractive material.

Use punctuation consistent with that of the compound and complex sentences.

Other Methods of Combining Ideas

1. Simple sentences can often be combined by using a **prepositional phrase,** a preposition followed by a noun or pronoun object.

    Dolly Parton wrote a song about a coat. The coat had many colors.

    Dolly Parton wrote a song about a coat *of many colors.*

2. To combine simple sentences, use an **appositive,** a noun phrase that immediately follows a noun or pronoun and renames it.

    Susan is the leading scorer on the team. Susan is a quick and strong player.

    Susan, *a quick and strong player,* is the leading scorer on the team.

3. Simple sentences can often be combined by dropping a repeated subject in the second sentence.

    Some items are too damaged for recycling. They must be disposed of.

    Some items are too damaged for recycling and must be disposed of.

4. Sentences can be combined by using a **participial phrase,** a group of words that includes a participle, which is a verblike word that usually ends in *-ing* or *-ed.*

    John rowed smoothly. He reached the shore.

    Rowing smoothly, John reached the shore.

✳ Variety in Sentences: Types, Order, Length, Beginnings

Do not bother to look for formulas in this section. Variety in sentences may be desirable for its own sake, to avoid dullness. However, it is more likely you will revise your essays for reasons that make good sense in the context of what you are writing. The following are some of the variations available to you.

Types

You have learned that all four types of sentences are sound. Your task as a writer is to decide which one to use for a particular thought. That decision may not be made until you revise your composition. Then you can choose on the basis of the relationship of ideas:

Simple: a single idea

Compound: two closely related ideas

Complex: one idea more important than the other

Compound-Complex: a combination of compound and complex

These types were all covered earlier in this handbook (p. 165).

Order

You will choose the order of parts and information according to what you want to emphasize. Typically the most emphatic location is at the end of any unit.

Length

Uncluttered and direct, short sentences commonly draw attention. But that focus occurs only when they stand out from longer sentences. Therefore, you would usually avoid a series of short sentences.

Beginnings

A long series of sentences with each beginning containing a subject followed by a verb may become monotonous. Consider beginning sentences in different ways:

With a prepositional phase: *In the distance* a dog barked.

**With a transitional connective (conjunctive adverb) such as *then, however,* or *therefore:* *Then* the game was over.

With a coordinating conjunction such as *and* or *but*: *But* no one moved for three minutes.

With a dependent clause: *Although he wanted a new Corvette,* he settled for a used Ford Taurus.

With an adverb: *Carefully* he removed the thorn from the lion's paw.

✳ Parallel Structure

Parallelism means balancing one structure with another of the same kind—nouns with nouns, verbs with verbs, adjectives (words that can describe nouns) with adjectives, adverbs (words that can describe verbs) with adverbs, and so forth.

> *Men, women,* and *children* [nouns] *enjoy* the show and *return* [verbs] each year.
>
> She fell *in love* and *out of love* [phrases] in a few seconds.
>
> *She fell in love with him,* and *he fell in love with her* [clauses].

1. Faulty parallel structure is awkward and draws unfavorable attention to what is being said.

   > *To talk* with his buddies and *eating* fast foods were his favorite pastimes. (The sentence should read *Talking . . .* and *eating* or *To talk . . .* and *to eat.*)

2. Some words signal parallel structure. All coordinating conjunctions (*for, and, nor, but, or, yet, so*) can give such signals.

   > The weather is hot *and* humid.
   >
   > He purchased a Dodger Dog, *but* I chose Stadium Peanuts.

3. Combination words also signal the need for parallelism or balance. The most common ones are *either/or, neither/nor, not only/but also, both/and,* and *whether/or.*

   > We will *either* win this game *or* go out fighting. (verb following each of the combination words)

✳ Omissions: When Parts Are Missing

Do not omit words that are needed to make your sentences clear and logical. Of the many types of undesirable constructions in which necessary words are omitted, the following are the most common.

1. **Subjects.** Do not omit a necessary subject in a sentence with two verbs.

> ILLOGICAL The cost of the car was $12,000 but would easily last me through college. (subject of last)
> LOGICAL The cost of the car was $12,000, but the car would easily last me through college.

2. **Verbs.** Do not omit verbs that are needed because of a change in the number of the subject or a change of tense.

> ILLOGICAL The bushes were trimmed and the grass mowed.
> LOGICAL The bushes were trimmed, and the grass was mowed.

> ILLOGICAL True honesty always has and always will be admired by most people. (tense)
> LOGICAL True honesty always has been and always will be admired by most people.

3. ***That* as a conjunction.** The conjunction *that* should not be omitted from a dependent clause if there is danger of misreading the sentence.

> MISLEADING We believed Eric, if not stopped, would hurt himself.
> CLEAR We believed that Eric, if not stopped, would hurt himself.

4. **Prepositions.** Do not omit prepositions in idiomatic phrases, in expressions of time, and in parallel phrases.

> ILLOGICAL Weekends the campus is deserted. (time)
> LOGICAL During weekends the campus is deserted.

> ILLOGICAL I have neither love nor patience with untrained dogs. (parallel phrases)
> LOGICAL I have neither love for nor patience with untrained dogs.

> ILLOGICAL Glenda's illness was something we heard only after her recovery. (preposition omitted)
> LOGICAL Glenda's illness was something we heard about only after her recovery.

✳ Verbs

The twelve verb tenses are shown in this section. The irregular verb *drive* is used as the example. (See pp. 224–225 for a list of irregular verbs.)

Simple Tenses
Present
I, we, you, they *drive.*
He, she, it *drives.*

May imply
a continuation from
past to future

Past
I, we, you, he, she, it, they *drove.*

Future
I, we, you, he, she, it,
they *will drive.*

Perfect Tenses
Present Perfect
I, we, you, they *have driven.*
He, she, it *has driven.*

Completed recently
in the past, may con-
tinue to the present

Past Perfect
I, we, you, he, she, it, they *had driven.*

Completed prior to a
specific time in the
past

Future Perfect
I, we, you, he, she, it, they *will have
driven.*

Will occur at a time
prior to a specific
time in the future

Progressive Tenses
Present Progressive
I *am driving.*
He, she, it *is driving.*
We, you, they *are driving.*

In progress now

Past Progressive
I, he, she, it *was driving.*
We, you, they *were driving.*

In progress in the
past

Future Progressive
I, we, you, he, she, it, they *will be
driving.*

In progress in the
future

Perfect Progressive Tenses

Present Perfect Progressive

I, we, you, they *have been driving.*
He, she, it *has been driving.*

In progress up to now

Past Perfect Progressive

I, we, you, he, she, it, they *had been driving.*

In progress before another event in the past

Future Perfect Progressive

I, we, you, he, she, it, they *will have been driving.*

In progress before another event in the future

Past Participles

The past participle uses the helping verbs *has, have,* or *had* along with the past tense of the verb. For regular verbs, whose past tense ends in *-ed,* the past participle form of the verb is the same as the past tense.

Following is a list of some common regular verbs, showing the base form, the past tense, and the past participle. (The base form can also be used with such helping verbs as *can, could, do, does, did, may, might, must, shall, should, will,* and *would.*)

Regular Verbs

Base Form (Present)	Past	Past Participle
ask	asked	asked
answer	answered	answered
cry	cried	cried
decide	decided	decided
dive	dived (dove)	dived
finish	finished	finished
happen	happened	happened
learn	learned	learned
like	liked	liked
love	loved	loved
need	needed	needed
open	opened	opened

Base Form (Present)	Past	Past Participle
start	started	started
suppose	supposed	supposed
walk	walked	walked
want	wanted	wanted

Whereas **regular verbs** are predictable—having an -*ed* ending for past and past-participle forms—**irregular verbs,** as the term suggests, follow no definite pattern.

Following is a list of some common irregular verbs, showing the base form (present), the past tense, and the past participle.

Irregular Verbs

Base Form (Present)	Past	Past Participle
arise	arose	arisen
awake	awoke (awaked)	awaked
be	was, were	been
become	became	become
begin	began	begun
bend	bent	bent
blow	blew	blown
break	broke	broken
bring	brought	brought
buy	bought	bought
catch	caught	caught
choose	chose	chosen
cling	clung	clung
come	came	come
creep	crept	crept
deal	dealt	dealt
do	did	done
drink	drank	drunk
drive	drove	driven
eat	ate	eaten
feel	felt	felt
fight	fought	fought
fling	flung	flung
fly	flew	flown
forget	forgot	forgotten
freeze	froze	frozen
get	got	got (gotten)

Base Form (Present)	Past	Past Participle
go	went	gone
grow	grew	grown
have	had	had
know	knew	known
lead	led	led
leave	left	left
lose	lost	lost
mean	meant	meant
read	read	read
ride	rode	ridden
ring	rang	rung
see	saw	seen
shine	shone	shone
shoot	shot	shot
sing	sang	sung
sink	sank	sunk
sleep	slept	slept
slink	slunk	slunk
speak	spoke	spoken
spend	spent	spent
steal	stole	stolen
stink	stank (stunk)	stunk
sweep	swept	swept
swim	swam	swum
swing	swung	swung
take	took	taken
teach	taught	taught
tear	tore	torn
think	thought	thought
throw	threw	thrown
wake	woke (waked)	woken (waked)
weep	wept	wept
write	wrote	written

"Problem" Verbs

The following pairs of verbs are especially troublesome and confusing: *lie* and *lay, sit* and *set,* and *rise* and *raise.* One way to tell them apart is to remember which word in each pair takes a direct object. A direct object answers the question *whom* or *what* in connection with a verb. The words *lay, raise,* and *set* take a direct object.

> He *raised* the window. (He *raised* what?)

Lie, rise, and *sit,* however, cannot take a direct object. We cannot, for example, say "He rose the window." In the following examples, the italicized words are objects.

Present Tense	Meaning	Past Tense	Past Participle	Example
lie	to rest	lay	lain	I lay down to rest.
lay	to place something	laid	laid	We laid the *books* on the table.
rise	to go up	rose	risen	The smoke rose quickly.
raise	to lift	raised	raised	She raised the *question.*
sit	to rest	sat	sat	He sat in the chair.
set	to place something	set	set	They set the *basket* on the floor.

Verb Tense

Verb tense is a word form indicating time. The rules about selecting a tense for certain kinds of writing are flexible. You should be consistent, however, changing tense only for a good reason.

Usually you should select the present tense to write about literature.

Moby Dick *is* a famous white whale.

Select the past tense to write about yourself (usually) or something historical (always).

I *was* eighteen when I *decided* I *was* ready for independence.

Subject-Verb Agreement

The basic principle of **subject-verb agreement** is that if the subject is singular, the verb should be singular, and if the subject is plural, the verb should be plural.

The *advantages* of that shoe *are* obvious.

There *are* many *reasons* for his poor work.

The *coach,* along with the players, *protests* the decision.

The *price* of those shoes *is* too high.

Voice

The **active voice** (subject, active verb, and object) is usually preferred over the **passive voice** (subject as the receiver of action, with doer unstated or at the end of a prepositional phrase).

ACTIVE   She read the book.

PASSIVE   The book was read by her.

⁎ Pronouns

A **pronoun** is a word that is used in place of a noun. **Case** is the form a pronoun takes as it fills a position in a sentence.

1. **Subjective pronouns** are *I, he,* and *she* (singular), and *we* and *they* (plural). *Who* can be either singular or plural.
   Subjective case pronouns can fill subject positions in a sentence.

   We dance in the park.

   It was *she* who spoke. (referring back to and meaning the same as the subject)

2. **Objective pronouns** are *me, him,* and *her* (singular); and *us* and *them* (plural). *Whom* can be either singular or plural.
   Objective case pronouns fill object positions.

   We saw *her* in the library. (object of verb)

   They gave the results to *us*—Judy and *me.* (object of a preposition)

3. Three techniques are useful for deciding what pronoun case to use.
   a. If you have a compound element (such as a subject or an object of a preposition), consider only the pronoun part.

   They will visit Jim and (I, me). (*Consider:* They will visit *me.*)

   b. If the next important word after *who* or *whom* in a statement is a noun or pronoun, the word choice will be *whom;* otherwise, it will be *who.* Disregard qualifier clauses such as *It seems* and *I feel.*

   The person *who* works hardest will win.

   The person *whom* judges like will win.

The person *who,* we think, worked hardest won. (ignoring the qualifier clause)

c. *Let's* is made up of the words *let* and *us* and means "you *let us*"; therefore, when you select a pronoun to follow it, consider the two original words and select another object word—*me.*

Let's you and *me* go to town.

4. A pronoun agrees with its antecedent in person, number, and gender.
   a. Avoid needless shifting in person, which means shifting in point of view, such as from *I* to *you.*

   INCORRECT   *I* tried but *you* couldn't persuade her to return.

   CORRECT   *I* tried but *I* couldn't persuade her to return.

   b. Most problems with pronoun-antecedent agreement involve number. The principles are simple: If the antecedent (the word the pronoun refers back to) is singular, use a singular pronoun. If the antecedent is plural, use a plural pronoun.

   Jim forgot *his* notebook.

   Many students cast *their* votes today.

   Someone lost *his* or *her* [not *their*] book.

   c. The pronoun should agree with its antecedent in gender if the gender of the antecedent is specific. Masculine and feminine pronouns are gender-specific: *he, him, she,* and *her.* Others are neuter: *I, we, me, us, it, they, them, who, whom, that,* and *which.* The words *who* and *whom* refer to people. *That* can refer to ideas, things, and people, but usually not to people. *Which* refers to ideas and things, but never to people. To avoid a perceived sex bias, most writers and speakers prefer to use *he or she* or *his or her* instead of just *he* or *his;* however, many writers simply make antecedents plural.

   Everyone should work until *he or she* drops.

   People should work until *they* drop.

✳ Adjectives and Adverbs

1. **Adjectives** modify (describe) nouns and pronouns and answer the questions *Which one? What kind?* and *How many?*
2. **Adverbs** modify verbs, adjectives, or other adverbs and answer the questions *How? Where? When?* and *To what degree?* Most words ending in *-ly* are adverbs.
3. If you settle for a common word such as *good* or a slang word such as *neat* to characterize something you like, you will be limiting your communication. The more precise the word, the better the communication. Keep in mind, however, that anything can be overdone; therefore, use adjectives and adverbs wisely and economically.
4. For making comparisons, most adjectives and adverbs have three different forms: the positive (one), the comparative (two), and the superlative (three or more).
   a. Adjectives
      ▪ Add *-er* to short adjectives (one or two syllables) to rank units of two.

         Julian is *kinder* than Sam.

      ▪ Add *-est* to short adjectives (one or two syllables) to rank units of more than two.

         Of the fifty people I know, Julian is the *kindest.*

      ▪ Add the word *more* before long adjectives to rank units of two.

         My hometown is *more beautiful* than yours.

      ▪ Add the word *most* before long adjectives to rank units of three or more.

         My hometown is the *most beautiful* in all America.

      ▪ Some adjectives are irregular in the way they change to show comparison: *good, better, best; bad, worse, worst.*
   b. Adverbs
      For most adverbs, use the word *more* before the comparative form (two) and the word *most* before the superlative form (three or more).

         Jim performed *skillfully.* (modifier)

         Joan performed *more skillfully* than Sam. (comparative modifier)

But Susan performed *most skillfully* of all. (superlative modifier)

5. Avoid double negatives. Words such as *no, not, none, nothing, never, hardly, barely,* and *scarcely* should not be combined.

> INCORRECT   I *don't* have *no* time for recreation.
>
> CORRECT   I have *no* time for recreation.
>
> CORRECT   I *don't* have time for recreation.

6. Do not confuse adjectives (*bad*) with adverbs (*badly*).

7. A modifier that gives information but doesn't refer to a word or group of words already in the sentence is called a **dangling modifier.**

> DANGLING   *Walking down the street,* a snake startled me.
>
> CORRECT   *Walking down the street, I* was startled by a snake.

8. A modifier that is placed so that it modifies the wrong word or words is called a **misplaced modifier.**

> MISPLACED   The sick man went to a doctor *with a high fever.*
>
> CORRECT   The sick man *with a high fever* went to a doctor.

✳ Avoiding Wordy Phrases

Certain phrases clutter sentences, consuming our time in writing and our readers' time in reading. Watch for wordy phrases as you revise and edit.

> WORDY   *Due to the fact that* he was unemployed, he had to use public transportation.
>
> CONCISE   *Because* he was unemployed, he had to use public transportation.
>
> WORDY   *Deep down inside* he believed that the Red Sox would win.
>
> CONCISE   He believed that the Red Sox would win.

Wordy	Concise
at the present time	now
basic essentials	essentials

blend together	blend
it is clear that	(delete)
due to the fact that	because
for the reason that	because
I felt inside	I felt
in most cases	usually
as a matter of fact	in fact
in the event that	if
until such time as	until
I personally feel	I feel
in this modern world	today
in order to	to
most of the people	most people
along the lines of	like
past experience	experience
at that point in time	then
in the final analysis	finally
in the near future	soon
have a need for	need
in this day and age	now

✳ **Punctuation**

1. The three marks of end punctuation are periods, question marks, and exclamation points.
   a. Periods
      Place a period after a statement.
      Place a period after common abbreviations.
      Use an ellipsis—three periods within a sentence and four periods at the end of a sentence—to indicate that words have been omitted from quoted material.

> He stopped walking and the buildings. . . . rose up out of the misty courtroom. . . . (James Thurber, "The Secret Life of Walter Mitty")

   b. Question marks
      Place a question mark at the end of a direct question.
      Use a single question mark in sentence constructions that contain a double question—that is, a quoted question following a question.

Mr. Martin said, "Did he say, 'Are we going?'"

Do *not* use a question mark after an indirect (reported) question.

She asked me what caused the slide.

  c. **Exclamation points**
     Place an exclamation point after a word or group of words that expresses strong feeling.
     Do not overwork the exclamation point. Do not use double exclamation points.

2. The comma is used essentially to separate and to set off sentence elements.

  a. Use a comma to separate main clauses joined by one of the coordinating conjunctions—*for, and, nor, but, or, yet, so.*

     We went to the game, *but* it was canceled.

  b. Use a comma after introductory dependent clauses and long introductory phrases (generally, four or more words is considered long).

     Before she and I arrived, the meeting was called to order.

  c. Use a comma to separate words, phrases, and clauses in a series.

     He ran *down the street, across the park, and into the arms* of his father.

  d. Use a comma to separate coordinate adjectives not joined by *and* that modify the same noun.

     I need a *sturdy, reliable* truck.

  e. Use a comma to separate sentence elements that might be misread.

     Inside, the dog scratched his fleas.

  f. Use commas to set off (enclose) nonessential (unnecessary for meaning of the sentence) words, phrases, and clauses.

     Maria, *who studied hard,* will pass.

  g. Use commas to set off parenthetical elements such as mild interjections (*oh, well, yes, no,* and others), most conjunctive adverbs (*however, otherwise, therefore, similarly, hence, on the other hand,* and *consequently,* but not *then, thus, soon, now,* and *also*), quotation indicators, and special abbreviations (*etc., i.e., e.g.,* and others).

> *Oh,* what a silly question! (mild interjection)
>
> It is necessary, *of course, to* leave now. (sentence modifier)
>
> We left early; *however,* we missed the train anyway, (conjunctive adverb)
>
> "When I was in school," *he said,* "I read widely." (quotation indicators)
>
> Books, papers, pens, *etc.,* were scattered on the floor. (The abbreviation *etc.,* however, should be used sparingly.)

h. Use commas to set off nouns used as direct address.

> Play it again, *Sam.*

i. Use commas to separate the numbers in a date.

> June *4, 1965,* is a day I will remember.

j. Use commas to separate the city from the state. No comma is used between the state and the ZIP code.

> Walnut, CA 91789

k. Use a comma following the salutation and the complementary closing in a letter (but in a business letter, use a colon after the salutation).

> Dear John,
>
> Sincerely,

l. Use a comma in numbers to set off groups of three digits. However, omit the comma in dates and in long serial numbers, page numbers, and street numbers.

> The total assets were *$2,000,000.*
>
> I was born in 1980.

3. The semicolon indicates a stronger division than the comma. It is used principally to separate independent clauses within a sentence.

a. Use a semicolon to separate independent clauses not joined by a coordinating conjunction.

> You must buy that car today; tomorrow will be too late.

b. Use a semicolon between two independent clauses joined by a conjunctive adverb (such as *however, otherwise, therefore, similarly, hence, on the other hand, then, consequently, accordingly, thus*).

> It was very late; *therefore,* I remained at the hotel.

4. Quotation marks bring special attention to words.
   a. Quotation marks are used principally to set off direct quotations. A direct quotation consists of material taken from the written work or the direct speech of others; it is set off by double quotation marks. Single quotation marks are used to set off a quotation within a quotation.

   > He said, "I don't remember if she said, 'Wait for me.'"

   b. Use double quotation marks to set off titles of shorter pieces of writing such as magazine articles, essays, short stories, short poems, one-act plays, chapters in books, songs, and separate pieces of writing published as part of a larger work.

   > The book *Literature: Structure, Sound, and Sense* contains a deeply moving poem titled "On Wenlock Edge."
   >
   > Have you read "The Use of Force," a short story by William Carlos Williams?
   >
   > My favorite Elvis song is "Don't Be Cruel."

   c. Punctuation with quotation marks follows definite rules.

   - A period or a comma is always placed *inside* the quotation marks.

     > Our assignment for Monday was to read Poe's "The Raven."
     >
     > "I will read you the story," he said. "It is a good one."

   - A semicolon or a colon is always placed *outside* the quotation marks.

     > He read Robert Frost's poem "Design"; then he gave the examination.

   - A question mark, an exclamation point, or a dash is placed *outside* the quotation marks when it applies to the entire sentence and *inside* the quotation marks when it applies to the material in quotation marks.

He asked, "Am I responsible for everything?" (quoted question within a statement)

Did you hear him say, "I have the answer"? (statement within a question)

Did she say, "Are we ready?" (question within a question)

She shouted, "Impossible!" (exclamation)

"I hope—that is, I—" he began. (dash)

5. Italics (slanting type) is used to call special attention to certain words or groups of words. In handwriting, such words are underlined.
   a. Italicize (underline) foreign words and phrases that are still listed in the dictionary as foreign.

   nouveau riche   Weltschmerz

   b. Italicize (underline) titles of books (except the Bible), long poems, plays, magazines, motion pictures, musical compositions, newspapers, works of art, names of aircraft, ships, and letters, figures, and words referred to by their own name.

   War and Peace   Apollo 12   leaving *o* out of *sophomore*

6. The dash is used when a stronger break than the comma is needed. It can also be used to indicate a break in the flow of thought and to emphasize words (less formal than the colon in this situation).

   Here is the true reason—but maybe you don't care.

   English, French, history—these are the subjects I like.

7. The colon is a formal mark of punctuation used chiefly to introduce something that is to follow, such as a list, a quotation, or an explanation.

   These cars are my favorites: Cadillac, Chevrolet, Buick, Oldsmobile, and Pontiac.

8. Parentheses are used to set off material that is of relatively little importance to the main thought of the sentence. Such material—numbers that designate items in a series, figures, supplementary material, and sometimes explanatory details—merely amplifies the main thought.

   The years of the era (1961–1973) were full of action.

Her husband (she had been married only a year) died last week.

9. Brackets are used within a quotation to set off editorial additions or corrections made by the person who is quoting.

Churchill said: "It [the Yalta Agreement] contained many mistakes."

10. The apostrophe is used with nouns and indefinite pronouns to show possession, to show the omission of letters and figures in contractions, and to form the plurals of letters, figures, and words referred to as words.

man's coat girls' clothes
you're (contraction of *you are*) five *and*'s

11. The hyphen brings two or more words together into a single compound word. Correct hyphenation, therefore, is essentially a spelling problem rather than one of punctuation. Because the hyphen is not used with any degree of consistency, consult your dictionary for current usage. Study the following as a beginning guide.
    a. Use a hyphen to separate the parts of many compound words.

    about-face go-between

    b. Use a hyphen between prefixes and proper names.

    all-American mid-November

    c. Use a hyphen to join two or more words used as a single adjective modifier before a noun.

    first-class service hard-fought game
    sad-looking mother

    d. Use a hyphen with spelled-out compound numbers up to ninety-nine and with fractions.

    twenty-six two-thirds

Note: Dates, street addresses, numbers requiring more than two words, chapter and page numbers, time followed directly by *a.m.* or *p.m.*, and figures after a dollar sign or before measurement abbreviations are usually written as figures, not words.

✳ Capitalization

In English, there are many conventions concerning the use of capital letters. Here are some of them.

1. Capitalize the first word of a sentence.
2. Capitalize proper nouns and adjectives derived from proper nouns.

- Names of persons
  Edward Jones

- Adjectives derived from proper nouns
  a Shakespearean sonnet   an English class

- Countries, nationalities, races, and languages
  Germany   English   Spanish   Chinese

- States, regions, localities, and other geographical divisions
  California   the Far East   the South

- Oceans, lakes, mountains, deserts, streets, and parks
  Lake Superior   Fifth Avenue   Sahara Desert

- Educational institutions, schools, and courses
  Santa Ana College   Math 3   Joe Hill School
  Rowland High School

- Organizations and their members
  Boston Red Sox   Boy Scouts   Audubon Society

- Corporations, governmental agencies or departments, and trade names
  U.S. Steel Corporation   Treasury Department
  White Memorial Library   Coke

- Calendar references such as holidays, days of the week, and months
  Easter   Tuesday   January

- Historic eras, periods, documents, and laws
  Declaration of Independence   Geneva Convention
  First Crusade   Romantic Age

3. Capitalize words denoting family relationships when they are used before a name or substituted for a name.

He walked with his nephew and Aunt Grace.

but

He walked with his nephew and his aunt.

Grandmother and Mother are away on vacation.

but

My grandmother and my mother are away on vacation.

4. Capitalize abbreviations after names.

Henry White Jr.   William Green, M.D.

5. Capitalize titles of essays, books, plays, movies, poems, magazines, newspapers, musical compositions, songs, and works of art. Do not capitalize short conjunctions and prepositions unless they come at the beginning or the end of the title.

Desire Under the Elms   *Terminator*
Last of the Mohicans   *Of Mice and Men*
"Blueberry Hill"

6. Capitalize any title preceding a name or used as a substitute for a name. Do not capitalize a title following a name.

Judge Stone   Alfred Stone, a judge
General Clark   Raymond Clark, a general
Professor Fuentes   Harry Jones, the former president

✳ Acknowledgments

Suzanne Britt, "Neat People vs. Sloppy People," from *Show and Tell*. Reprinted by permission of the author.

Benedict Carey, "The Roots of Temptation," *Los Angeles Times*, October 20, 2003. Copyright © 2003, Los Angeles Times. Reprinted by permission.

John Cordell, "The Ballad of Anna Banana" and "Though Blindness Came to Grandpa, He Could See" from *Oklahoma, My Sweet Sorrow*. Copyright © 1999, by Lee Brandon.

Steven Doloff, "The Opposite Sex" is reprinted by permission of the author.

Suzanne Fields, "Let Granny Drive If She Can." It was originally published in the *Washington Times*, Op-Ed, July 24, 2003. Reprinted by permission of the author.

Joyce Gallagher, "The Messy Are in Denial" and "A Modest Proposal: Guys Shouldn't Drive Till 25," reprinted with permission of the author.

John Gray, Excerpt from "Mr. Fix-It and the Home-Improvement Committee" from *Men Are from Mars, Women Are from Venus* by John Gray. Copyright © 1992 by John Gray. Reprinted by permission of HarperCollins Publishers Inc.

Gina Greenlee, "No Tears for Frankie" from *The New York Times* Magazine, June 10, 2001. Reprinted by permission of the author.

Donna Brown Hogarty, "How to Deal with a Difficult Boss." Reprinted with permission of the author from the July 1993 *Reader's Digest*.

Molly Ivins, "Get a Knife, Get a Dog, but Get Rid of Guns" from *Nothin' but Good Times Ahead* by Molly Ivins, copyright © 1993 by Molly Ivins. Used by permission of Random House, Inc.

Stephen Lemons, "Creepin' While You're Sleepin'," *New Times Los Angeles*, May 4, 2000. Reprinted by permission of the author.

John Leo, "Bully, Bully." *U.S. News and World Report*, May 21, 2001, vol. 130, issue 20, p. 150. Copyright 2001 *U.S. News and World Report*. Reprinted with permission.

John R. Lott Jr., "Letting Teachers Pack Guns Will Make America's Schools Safer," *Los Angeles Times*, July 13, 2003. Reprinted by permission of the author.

Erica Monfred, "Coworkers from Hell and How to Cope," *Cosmopolitan*, February 1, 1997. Reprinted by permission of the author.

Katherine S. Newman, "Low Wages, High Skills" excerpt from *No Shame in My Game* by Katherine S. Newman. Copyright © 1999 by Russell Sage Foundation. Used by permission of Alfred A. Knopf, a division of Random House, Inc.

Ian Robertson, "Romantic Love, Courtship, and Marriage," from *Sociology* by Ian Robertson. © 1971, 1981, 1987 by Worth Publishers. Used with permission.

Anne Roiphe, "Why Marriages Fail," is reprinted by permission of International Creative Management, Inc. Copyright © 1993 by Anne Roiphe.

Eric Schlosser, "Behind the Counter" from *Fast Food Nation* by Eric Schlosser. Copyright © 2001 by Eric Schlosser. Reprinted by permission of Houghton Mifflin Company. All rights reserved.

Irwin Shaw, "The Girls in Their Summer Dresses," from *Five Decades* by Irwin Shaw. Reprinted with permission. © Irwin Shaw. All rights reserved.

Robert J. Trotter, "How Do I Love Thee? Counting the Ways," from Sharon S. Brehm, Saul M. Kassin, and Steven Fein, Houghton Mifflin Company, *Social Psychology*, 5/e, 2002, pp. 327–328. Copyright © 2002 by Houghton Mifflin Company. Reprinted with permission.

✳ Index